THE MADONNA
AN ANTHOLOGY

THE NATIVITY

Andrea della Robbia

THE MADONNA

AN ANTHOLOGY

Selected and Edited by

SIR JAMES MARCHANT, K.B.E.

Editor of the 'Anthology of Jesus,' etc.

WITH AN INTRODUCTION ON
THE MADONNA IN ART BY

SIR CHARLES HOLMES, K.C.V.O.

DIRECTOR OF THE NATIONAL GALLERY

WITH NUMEROUS ILLUSTRATIONS

LONGMANS, GREEN AND CO.

LONDON • NEW YORK • TORONTO

1928

LONGMANS, GREEN AND CO. Ltd.
39 PATERNOSTER ROW, LONDON, E.C. 4
6 OLD COURT HOUSE STREET, CALCUTTA
53 NICOL ROAD, BOMBAY
167 MOUNT ROAD, MADRAS

LONGMANS, GREEN AND CO.
55 FIFTH AVENUE, NEW YORK
221 EAST 20TH STREET, CHICAGO
TREMONT TEMPLE, BOSTON
210 VICTORIA STREET, TORONTO

Made in Great Britain

Now there stood by the cross of Jesus his mother.

When Jesus saw his mother, and the disciple standing by, whom he loved, he saith unto his mother, Woman, behold thy son!

Then saith he to the disciple, Behold thy mother! And from that hour that disciple took her unto his own home.

St. John xix. 25-27.

CONTENTS

LIST OF ILLUSTRATIONS

LIST OF ILLUSTRATIONS xiii

To face page

THE MADONNA IN ART

I

For some sixteen centuries the artists of Europe have concerned themselves with the portrayal of the Madonna. Many of these representations, produced when artistic experience was limited and materials were imperfect, have an interest for the archæologist rather than for the artist. Many more, indeed the vast majority, must be regarded in the light of devotional symbols, echoing perhaps some fine earlier presentation, but entirely lacking in that intensity of feeling and creative personal craftsmanship which distinguish the true work of art. The plaster statuette of modern commerce and the ordinary Byzantine ikon may stand for two extreme types of this derivative imagery. But the Madonna has also been a subject for almost all the great artists of Catholic Europe during the Middle Ages and the Renaissance, so that even when we set aside altogether the works that are primitive or conventional, the sum total of the paintings and sculpture that we have to consider is no less enormous than it is important.

When we attempt a general survey of this greatly reduced but still vast and varied artistic field, one line of thought is inevitably thrust upon us. We are driven to compare the results obtained respectively by

b

the painter and the sculptor. The mosaicist has a province of his own, which once or twice, as in the great apsidal Madonna at Torcello, yields a result of incomparable majesty. But for the most part the rivalry is one between painting and sculpture, and the more earnestly we try to decide the issue, the stronger do the claims of sculpture seem to become.

It is doubtful whether the result would be quite the same in the case of the life of our Lord. His mission on earth was primarily concerned with the multitude. The dramatic events in it usually took place either in the presence of the Apostles or of the people who assembled to see and to hear Him. For such a life, surrounded with such a variety of human interest, painting was in general the appropriate artistic medium. Sculpture departs from its province, and loses its native monumental simplicity, when it attempts to present a large number of figures. So the life and person of Christ can be treated with complete success by the sculptor only when he is content to select a few simple significant gestures, or to become altogether symbolic.

The life of the Madonna was wholly different. Once or twice, as in her presence at the Marriage at Cana or the Crucifixion, she is definitely one of a considerable company. But usually her life, legendary or historical, was passed in seclusion. Several of its most popular and significant phases, the Annunciation, her motherhood, her sorrow over the body of her Son, her glorification as the Queen of Heaven, need no more than two or three figures for their com-

MADONNA AND CHILD

XIIth Century

plete presentation.   Here, therefore, sculpture has its
perfect opportunity, and though the greatest painters
of the world have set themselves to the same problems,
and have solved them triumphantly, the triumph has
usually been attained by conforming so far as possible
to the conditions of simple massing and solid rendering
which are characteristic of sculpture.   But with sculpture, at least with the best sculpture of Italy and
France, we get these qualities naturally, with an addition of convincing substance and varied all-round
delicacy and character which no representation in the
flat can attain.   Hence it comes that the completely
satisfying presentations of the Madonna, with or without the Child, are at least as numerous in sculpture as
they are in painting.   As the scene becomes more
animated, the stage more crowded, painting attains
the mastery : most conspicuously, of course, when the
setting is removed from the earth to the skies, and the
Madonna is encircled with filmy clouds and radiant
glories, amid all the hosts of heaven.   Such effects
cannot well be cut in stone or marble.   Painting alone
may do them justice, so that any iconography of the
Madonna must necessarily be imperfect which does
not take both arts into account, and discriminate
exactly where each most completely fills its particular
function.

   These matters of design assume a still more prac-
tical importance when we think of them in connexion
with book illustration.   There the elaborate composition which fills so majestically the wall of some great
church or palace has to be presented in miniature.   A

few square inches may have to stand for as many square yards. Only the very simplest designs can stand the test of such a reduction. All the rest suffer, and suffer in proportion to their complexity. This is particularly noticeable in the case of the human face : all refinements of expression and character being necessarily lost when the scale is unduly diminished. And in a book like this it is just those refinements which count the most. I have therefore limited, for the most part, the choice of illustrations to those which stand the test of reduction tolerably well. This has involved the omission of many noble things. Other fine things are omitted as being so familiar that they have lost some of their first freshness for us. An element of surprise is essential, I believe, to full enjoyment of art in any form. A poem or melody loses no small part of its charm when, from frequent repetition, we come to know it too thoroughly. That charm we cannot recover until partial forgetfulness has intervened to give the attraction of novelty to a further hearing.[1]

II

Legend and theology have combined to amplify and adorn the scanty references in the Bible to the

[1] Those who are inclined to pursue the subject further will find a wealth of material in Mrs. Jameson's well-known book. *La Madonna*, by Commendatore Adolfo Venturi (Milano : Hoepli, 1900), is a superb album of illustrative material, mostly Italian. For France, the two admirable volumes of M. Emile Mâle, *L'Art Religieux du XIIIme Siècle en France* and *L'Art Religieux de la Fin du Moyen Âge en France* (Paris : Armand Colin), will be found no less indispensable than they are lucid and interesting.

Mother of Jesus.   So in the arts, which have followed and illustrated each phase of these accretions, Mary the Virgin has come to occupy a place no less prominent than her Son.   Nearly two thousand years have passed since the expiration of her life on earth, and for the first half of that period the record is comparatively simple.   The early Christian Church was pre-occupied with anticipations of immortality.   Images of the Good Shepherd who had given His life for His sheep, of the Martyrs who were now united with Him in glory, and emblems of the happiness of the blessed dead, predominate in the Catacombs.   The sole surviving records of the Virgin for the first three centuries of the Christian era are a painting of the Madonna and Child with the prophet Isaiah, and a representation of the Adoration of the Magi.   The Madonna whom Isaiah greets is presented as a plain human mother, without the least attempt at idealization, and with no apparent devotional significance.

That significance came at the end of the fourth century as an indirect result of the fierce controversy which took place over the mystery of the Incarnation. To Theodore of Mopsuestia we may owe the opinion that the Child born of Mary was an ordinary human being with whom at birth the divinity was united. This opinion, formulated by the patriarch Nestorius, was opposed at the Council of Ephesus in 431 by Cyril of Alexandria.   Cyril's followers won the day. Nestorius was condemned as a heretic, and insistence upon the divine birth of the Son made the glorification of the Mother of God a necessity for the orthodox.

Elevation to the supreme place among created beings led to veneration of the Virgin under two aspects. In the earlier of these she is represented with her Son as a devotional image, a visible symbol of protest against the Nestorian heresy. Then as the memory of ancient controversies grew dim, the association of the Mother and the Child loses its old doctrinal significance, and is gradually humanized, developing at last into those human and intimate groups, those 'Holy Families,' upon which the painters and sculptors of the later Middle Ages and the Renaissance lavished their utmost power.

The condemnation of the Nestorian heresy had another consequence. The perfection of the Mother involved as a necessary prelude that she herself should be born exempt from all human frailty. So the idea of the Immaculate Conception came into being, a doctrine which by the close of the fifteenth century had attained widespread popularity and acceptance. This approval henceforth was reflected in the arts, although it was not until 1854 that the doctrine was formally pronounced to be an article of faith.

In her second aspect the Virgin is the glorified Queen of Heaven, surrounded it may be with Saints and Angels, crowned by her divine Son, or pleading with Him as Intercessor for humanity when He comes to judge the World. This benign side of her nature is emphasized in the Madonna of Mercy who extends her cloak to shelter the poor and suffering, and most

JOACHIM'S DREAM

Giotto

particularly in connexion with death. As the Mater Dolorosa sorrowing at the foot of the Cross, or composing with the dead body of her Son a *Pietà* or image of supreme Pity, she has become the symbol of consolation for human grief no less generally than she has by her motherhood become the symbol of maternal love. And it would be hard to decide which of these two symbols has the more profoundly affected the arts. We can only recognize that no other themes have hitherto stimulated the painters and sculptors of Europe to any such lofty achievement.

In addition to these doctrinal or devotional aspects of the Madonna, the incidents of her life provided a wealth of picturesque material. The relatively scanty references in the canonical Gospels were soon augmented by the apocryphal Gospels and ancient popular tradition. Round the childhood of the Virgin, like that of Christ, legend had accumulated from the third century onwards. But it was not till the end of the thirteenth century that these legends and apocryphal Gospels were summarized in a definite shape which any painter could utilize. Thanks to those encyclopedias of tradition, the ' Miroir Historique ' of Vincent de Beauvais and the ' Golden Legend ' of Jacopo de Voragine, Joachim and Anna, the parents of the Virgin, are become as familiar in art as the personages of canonical scripture. Hardly less familiar are the legendary incidents of the Virgin's existence after the Crucifixion, and her Assumption in the presence of the Apostles, patriarchs, and angels. So the student of art is presented with a more or less consistent and consecutive series of episodes, which can easily be differentiated. His difficulties begin only when he has to deal with specialized or local cults, or with the infinite variety of aspects in which painters and sculptors have interpreted the relation of the Mother to the Son.

III

JOACHIM AND ANNA

The legend of Joachim and Anna, the parents of the Virgin, is so rich with pictorial incident that from the thirteenth to the fifteenth century it was a general favourite with artists. Of the numerous episodes, none has produced a more delightful composition than the appearance of the Angel to Joachim in his retirement among the shepherds, as recorded by Giotto in the Eremitani Chapel at Padua. The meeting of husband and wife at the Golden Gate is less an opportunity for the picturesque than for the expression of intimate feeling, and in this no representation is more tender than that by the Maître de Moulins, a work remarkable also for its startling Pre-Raphaelite modernity of tone. For the legend as a whole, Giotto at Padua, with Taddeo Gaddi and Ghirlandajo in Florence, count as the most famous illustrators.

THE BIRTH OF THE VIRGIN

With the Birth of the Virgin the artistic horizon widens. In the North, Altdorfer's exquisite and fanciful picture at Augsburg perhaps deserves the first place.   In Italy the subject serves as a background to one of the most exquisite of Filippo Lippi's Madonnas : Ghirlandajo uses it for the most notable of those hybrid compositions through which great ladies of the day stroll unheeding and unheeded ; while Andrea del Sarto, perhaps more consistently, treats it as if it were an event altogether contemporary with himself.

THE CHILDHOOD OF THE VIRGIN

The Presentation of the Virgin, made notable in the legend by her ascent of the steps of the Temple, was successfully treated in painting by Giotto at Padua, as by Taddeo Gaddi and Giovanni da Milano in Florence.   Orcagna too, in Or San Michele, makes a daring effort to tell the story in sculpture, but for once the difficulties of the subject prove too much for that masterly designer.   The Venetians, however, saw what opportunities of pageantry the scene presented. Carpaccio's admirable painting in the Brera, and Cima's composition at Dresden, lead up to Titian's vast canvas at the Accademia.   Then Tintoretto in S. Maria dell' Orto treats it with his full power, and produces one of the most compact and imposing of all his designs.

With this subject we may couple another, the Education of the Virgin, which was much more rarely painted by the earlier artists.   Rubens and Murillo, however, made it the subject of well-known compositions, and ' The Girlhood of Mary, Virgin ' was one of the very first works in which Rossetti displayed his youthful genius when the Pre-Raphaelite Brotherhood was founded.

THE MARRIAGE OF THE VIRGIN

The Marriage of the Virgin admitted considerable variety of treatment. Orcagna's relief in Or San Michele is a superb example of how such a subject can be reduced to the simplest possible terms with no loss of impressiveness. A remarkable fresco by Lorenzo da Viterbo goes to the opposite extreme, and surrounds the event with a crowd of lively figures in contemporary dress. The youthful Raphael with his usual serene judgment chooses just so much of the crowd as will illustrate the story of the disappointed suitors, and then unites them with the three chief personages in the famous composition in the Brera, at once so spacious and so compact. Lastly, Greco, in a picture at Bucarest, takes the ceremony and handles it with a simplicity not less than Orcagna's, and an airy grace which he too seldom displays.

THE VIRGIN ALONE

The significance of the Virgin begins with the recognition of her importance as a mother, so that it is only at certain periods and in certain aspects that she is represented without the Son. But as intercessor for man, as the 'Madonna orante,' she soon became a familiar figure, though less familiar and conspicuous than as the Queen of Heaven. At the end of the thirteenth century the human side of her

THE BIRTH OF THE VIRGIN
Altdorfer

nature was developed, so that afterwards it is chiefly as the protectress of the poor and humble, and as the perfect example of devotion or of sorrow, that she is found alone. Piero della Francesca at Borgo San Sepolcro gives us an imposing and typical specimen of the Madonna della Misericordia ; Sassoferrato in a later age popularized the bowed head of the Virgin in Prayer, creating indeed a type to which devotional images of the Madonna still frequently conform.

THE ANNUNCIATION

Of the countless paintings and sculptures of the Annunciation, as of other scenes which for centuries past have occupied all the great artists of Christendom, it is impossible in this place to treat in detail. The sculptors of France, as at Rheims, and of Italy— Donatello, Andrea della Robbia, Guglielmo da Pisa, and, on a lower plane, that surprising realist Antonello Gagini—have handled the theme with such exquisite insight and refinement that the painters must yield them precedence. Yet the ethereal charm of Fra Angelico and of Simone Martini, Botticelli's Virgin almost swooning at the wonder of the message, the slender figures of Baldovinetti and Bianchi Ferrari, the demure splendours of Cossa and Crivelli, when once seen are not easily forgotten. Titian, Tintoretto, and Veronese fail, I think, to compensate by vigour for what their conceptions lack in gentleness. The spirit of the scene is actually better preserved by the sophisticated Orazio Gentileschi, in his painting at

Turin, and by Rossetti. Indeed the example of the Venetians, and of Greco and Rubens after them, conclusively proves that the Annunciation is one of the themes which is too delicate to endure the imposition of drama or rhetoric upon its native virginal freshness.

THE VISITATION

In the case of the Visitation again, sculpture can set the superbly reverent group of Andrea della Robbia against the proudest efforts of painting. Andrea Pisano on the door of the Baptistry at Florence comes near to a similar triumph. And yet in painting we can turn at once to the noble and familiar design of Albertinelli, one of the few instances in which a minor master equals or surpasses greater men, and to the massive figures of Tintoretto on the S. Rocco staircase.

At this point in the legendary narrative occur the episodes representing the doubts of Joseph, and the ordeal successfully borne by himself and the Virgin. These episodes practically disappear from art after the twelfth century, as being no doubt but ambiguous aids to devotion, and so have left us no very precious graphic memorial of their existence.

THE NATIVITY

The representations of the Nativity present one well-marked difference. In the earlier paintings and sculptures the Virgin reclines on a bed in Oriental fashion. Giotto, Duccio, and Nicolo Pisano follow this ancient tradition. Then, about 1340, a new

imagery is introduced with Taddeo Gaddi and Bernardo
Daddi. The appurtenances of a normal birth disappear, perhaps because the Nativity when so presented seemed to lose something of its spiritual wonder,
and to be hardly different in essentials from the birth
of the Virgin. However this may be, the new presentation was adopted universally, and the figure of
the Virgin kneeling in prayer over the Child lying
before her became the recognized symbol of the
divine birth. The two Della Robbias have left
us exquisite renderings in that blue-and-white ware
which so admirably suggests the celestial purity of the
mother : the treatment of the subject in painting has
a more varied loveliness. To understand this we need
not go outside the walls of our own National Gallery,
where the 'Nativities' of Botticelli, of Piero della
Francesca, and of Geertgen tot Sint Jans are famous
and familiar treasures. With these the fine picture
by Filippo Lippi at Berlin deserves to be placed. In
Correggio's picture at Dresden the luminous night
effect of Geertgen is brilliantly elaborated. A little
panel by William Blake goes to the opposite extreme
of simplicity. Here there is no display of light and
shade or colour, but the artist, just like some primitive
sculptor, has so concentrated his fancy upon the
spiritual side of the event that, though we may smile
at his quaint imagery, we are satisfied with it.

THE ADORATION OF THE MAGI

Few artists have been able to resist the splendid
pageantry that the Adoration of the Magi admits and

suggests. The French sculptor of the Cloister of the Choir of Notre Dame, and Orcagna, as usual, in Florence succeed in reducing the episode to its plain elements, but among painters Memling at Bruges is almost alone in preserving complete simplicity. Pieter Brueghel's half-satiric rendering in the National Gallery—he had good reason for hating kings—is also broad and majestic. Mabuse, hard by, goes to the other extreme. Botticelli, too, uses the subject to introduce all manner of delightful if irrelevant detail. For Leonardo the Adoration becomes a symbol of the spiritual and intellectual attitude of humanity towards religion. For Rubens, as with Mabuse, it is a superb spectacle. Gentile Bellini is one of the few who, while keeping to the elaborate processional treatment, succeeds in endowing his figures with the spirit of the mystical East. With these wistful stately Orientals we may contrast the rude, skin-clad shepherds who pay their homage so devoutly in Ribera's fine picture at the Louvre.

THE PURIFICATION

In treating the Purification, Orcagna once more achieves a triumphant simplicity, similar to that of Giotto's fresco at Padua. At Venice, Carpaccio's large panel in the Academy is more favoured perhaps for the charming little angels who make music in the foreground than for the main episode. Mantegna's two pictures of the Presentation and the Circumcision at Berlin and Florence are among the finest Italian versions, while Rembrandt's etching with its sugges-

THE MARRIAGE OF THE VIRGIN

Orcagna

tion of grandeur, splendour, and mystery has a place
by itself in Northern Art.

THE FLIGHT INTO EGYPT

Of the compositions by Tintoretto in the Scuola
di San Rocco, that representing the Flight into Egypt
is one of the most notable, in that the journey is
invested with an atmosphere of marvel and romance
which simpler compositions lack.   Holman Hunt's
' Triumph of the Innocents ' is an interesting attempt
in modern times to recapture something of this feeling.
Among simpler designs, that of Murillo in the Palazzo
Bianco at Genoa is one of the finest, while Giotto,
Fra Angelico, and the French Sculptor of Notre Dame
may be named in connexion with more primitive
methods.   William Blake has left a fine composition
of the same type.

THE REST ON THE FLIGHT INTO EGYPT

The Flight into Egypt is traditionally associated with several miracles, of which that concerned
with the palm tree which bent and offered its fruit
makes the most frequent appearance in art.   But
usually the Repose of the Holy Family on their
flight is the subject chosen, and becomes a favourite
excuse for landscape, especially with Northern artists
like Joachim Patinir and his school.   Two German
artists go further.   Altdorfer in the picture at Berlin
seats the Virgin and Child by a fountain in which
child angels gambol and splash, while Dürer in his
famous print employs similar angels to collect and

store the chips from Joseph's adze. The Virgin close by and the Child in a cradle are tended by a second angelic group. A striking design by Caravaggio in the Doria Gallery, and the attractive paintings by Van Dyck at Munich and in the Hermitage, are among the best of the later renderings.

THE MADONNA AND CHILD

As we have seen, the association of the Mother with the Child was a necessary result of the condemnation of the Nestorians. So during the fifth century the image of the Mother of God, of the Madonna with her divine Son, became the symbol of orthodoxy. Gradually the importance of the Mother increased, until the popularity of this symbol was rivalled by that in which the Madonna was represented as the Queen of Heaven. By the fourteenth century her worship had grown more intimate. The human side of her motherhood was emphasized by intimate presentations of maternal love, extending into countless ' Holy Families ' which it is impossible in this place to enumerate, or even to classify. St. Joseph, St. John the Baptist, and St. Anne are the most frequent attendants upon the Madonna and Child : the mystical marriage of St. Catherine is another favourite accompaniment. We may be proud to possess in the ' Chichester Roundel,' of the first half of the thirteenth century, a proof that England was then the equal of any other artistic nation. Here the crowned Virgin and the Child embrace with a passionate absorption for which there are few parallels.

The apsidal mosaic at Torcello is perhaps the most imposing relic of the Madonna as Queen of Heaven. The French cathedral sculptures, like Donatello's extraordinary bronze at Padua, illustrate the transition from the regal to the maternal conception. Masaccio's Madonna at Trafalgar Square also retains much of the awe-inspiring divine ideal : it revives in the austere Madonnas of Michelangelo, so remote from all earthly tenderness. But the charm of human motherhood gained the day swiftly and almost universally. Raphael has been so long accepted as the perfect exponent of the theme that modern taste has turned to less familiar artists, among whom the Italian sculptors of the Quattrocento have an honourable place. With Rembrandt the human element is pressed sometimes to the verge of caricature.[1] With Rubens and Van Dyck mundane opulence or mundane elegance appear, and the latter quality finally overwhelms any touch of genuine feeling which later artists may have possessed.

CHRIST AMONG THE DOCTORS

Of the various representations of Christ among the Doctors, none are more convincing than the two little etchings by Rembrandt (Hind, 257 and 277). Here that master-psychologist had a subject to his liking, and the characteristics of the disputants are rendered with his full power and insight. The Madonna does not appear in either plate, but Rembrandt has recorded her visit in another etching

[1] As in the etching of 'The Virgin and Child in the Clouds' (Hind, 186).

d

(H. 276), in which Christ is shown returning homeward with His parents, the light of conflict still burning in His eyes. Rembrandt's types are rustic indeed
compared with those of the Italians, but as interpreta-
tions of human feeling they are incomparable.

CHRIST TAKING LEAVE OF HIS MOTHER

The crowded stage of the Marriage at Cana again
leaves but little room for the Madonna, so it is
in simple compositions, like that of Giotto at Padua,
that we are most definitely made aware of her presence.
But with this scene we may group another, far more
rarely delineated, but then so nobly as to deserve a
place in any study of the Madonna however concise.
In his print of Christ taking leave of His Mother,
Dürer attains to a dignity and pathos which even
Giovanni Bellini, the supreme master, I think, of such
noble sorrows, has never excelled. To this wonder
succeeds another. Just about six years later (1512)
Correggio treated the same subject with a beauty and
tenderness surpassing even Dürer's, and the picture,
thanks to the generosity of Sir Joseph Duveen, is
now among the treasures of the National Gallery. A
more affecting prelude to the scenes of the Passion it
would be difficult to conceive.

THE PROCESSION TO CALVARY

Like the Marriage at Cana the Procession to
Calvary as usually seen is too crowded with figures to
leave any prominent place for the Madonna. Only
in a half-symbolic treatment like that of Fra Angelico

THE VIRGIN AND CHILD

English, c. 1250

in San Marco can the connexion of the Mother and the Son be accorded prominence. Elsewhere she is enveloped by the train of soldiers and sightseers.

THE CRUCIFIXION

And in the ordinary representations of the Crucifixion she fares little better. But there are striking exceptions : as when with St. John the Beloved Disciple she is left alone by her dying Son. Of such pictures, that by Antonello da Messina in the National Gallery is one of the most majestic. In the ' Crucifixion ' by Matthias Grünewald at Colmar the conception is more passionate, and the Virgin swoons in the arms of the distracted St. John with a ghastly realism which recalls Goya. With this terrifying veracity we may contrast the serene resignation and solitary spacious landscape of Perugino in S. Maria Maddalena de' Pazzi.

THE DESCENT FROM THE CROSS

The majority of the great painters, from Fouquet in his miniature at Chantilly to Rubens in the vast canvas at Antwerp, have painted the Descent from the Cross. But they have almost invariably been so occupied with the problems of design, and of figures under intensive physical stress, which the scene entails, that the personages become hardly more than artistic accessories. Hence the various versions, while they generally include a figure of the Madonna, do not add anything new to our ideas of her personality.

THE ENTOMBMENT

With the Entombment it is otherwise. Though the Madonna's place in Donatello's marvellous relief at Padua is relatively unimportant, this unimportance is the exception. Her swooning figure is the nucleus of the group to the right in Raphael's famous but laboured composition in the Borghese : her blue robe is the unforgettable colour note of Titian's picture in the Prado. Caravaggio in the Vatican treated the subject with extraordinary power : it inspires Rembrandt to two of his most masterly etchings (H. 215 and H. 281). I know not whether to admire more the tragic little procession of the former, or the superb later design with the figures at work under the lamp-lit sepulchral vault. Nor can we overlook the realistic groups in painted terra-cotta of which examples can be seen at Modena and in certain places in France. The ' Saint Sepulchre' of Chaource is perhaps the most famous.

MATER DOLOROSA

Closely allied to the subject of the Entombment is that of the Madonna mourning over the dead body of her Son, the subject commonly catalogued as a *Pietà*, an image of Pity, the pity of all mothers for all dead sons, of which in its simplest form the symbol is the Mater Dolorosa, the Mother of all Sorrows. Of the primitive representations, that which has recently been removed to a place of honour in the Louvre from the convent at Villeneuve les Avignon is perhaps the most poignant.   The Florentine and Roman painters have not the same intensity ; in this they are altogether surpassed by the Venetians — Giovanni Bellini in particular.   But even Bellini has to share honours here with the young Buonconsiglio, whose picture at Vicenza is an altogether noble work.   Still more daring is the great picture by the aged Titian in the Venice Academy, where the silent grief of the Madonna is contrasted with the passionate outburst of the Magdalen.   In the next century Guido at Bologna, borrowing perhaps from one of Raphael's designs, gives us a majestic if somewhat sophisticated figure. Poussin at Dublin is no less impressive, and perhaps more genuine.   Though there is a noble bronze group by Donatello in the Victoria and Albert Museum, the supreme sculptor of the *Pietà* is Michelangelo. His early masterpiece in St. Peter's, with its youthful Madonna and polished surfaces, is perhaps more popular, but is certainly less powerful than the solemn group which he carved in extreme old age for the Duomo at Florence, or than that in the Rondanini Palace at Rome, where the Mother sustains and caresses the wasted body of her Son.

THE ASCENSION

Artists appear to have found difficulty in presenting the Ascension, perhaps because the figure of the risen Christ in mid-air and the crowd of disciples below necessarily involve a certain division of the spectators' interest.   Giotto at Padua, and Mantegna in the Uffizi, are among the few who have mastered this technical difficulty.

THE DEATH OF THE VIRGIN

A powerful rendering of the Death of the Virgin by Hugo van der Goes was a prominent feature in the Flemish Exhibition of January 1927. A small painting in the National Gallery (possibly an earlier work by the same master, No. 658) has no less intensity, to which the tiny sunlit landscape in the background makes an admirable contrast. In Mantegna's version in the Prado the landscape is still more important. Outside the great window a wide expanse of water provides a release from the sorrows of the death-bed, and a consolation for them, as a strain of gentle music might do. Caravaggio in the Louvre is dramatic, as we should expect from him; Rembrandt in his well-known print opens the bedchamber to the angelic host: but neither, I think, touches us so profoundly as does Mantegna.

THE ASSUMPTION OF THE VIRGIN

It is difficult to think of the Assumption of the Virgin without immediately recalling Titian's picture at Venice, so generally has that great work been recognized as the accepted pictorial rendering of the subject.

THE CORONATION OF THE VIRGIN

The Coronation of the Virgin offers a far wider choice. Fra Angelico has left us two noble pictures

THE MARRIAGE AT CANA

Giotto

in the Uffizi and the Louvre. Enguerrand Charonton at Villeneuve has converted the subject into one of the few surviving masterpieces of early French Art. Fra Filippo Lippi and Botticelli in two pictures at Florence reach their highest standard. Countless minor painters and sculptors have transformed it into a thing of beauty. Finally, in the Prado we may notice how a composition on a small scale by Greco (Pablo Bosch Collection) is borrowed by Velazquez and expanded into one of the most striking and famous of his later pictures.

With the representation of this subject we might perhaps group the paintings and sculptures which represent the Madonna and Child in their celestial aspect when surrounded by Saints and Angels, and the numerous pictures symbolizing the doctrine of the Immaculate Conception, of which Murillo is the most famous maker. The ramifications of the theme are so infinite that no exact classification is possible, or perhaps desirable, although it is to this indeterminate region that some of the loveliest of all the representations of the Madonna, like Botticelli's ' Magnificat ' in Florence, must be referred.

THE BIRTH OF THE VIRGIN

Andrea del Sarto

PROLOGUE

THE INCARNATION

St. John.

In the beginning was the Word, and the Word was with God, and the Word was God.

The same was in the beginning with God.

All things were made by him ; and without him was not any thing made that was made.

In him was life ; and the life was the light of men.

And the light shineth in darkness ; and the darkness comprehended it not. . . .

That was the true Light, which lighteth every man that cometh into the world.

He was in the world, and the world was made by him, and the world knew him not.

He came unto his own, and his own received him not.

But as many as received him, to them gave he power to become the sons of God, even to them that believe on his name :

Which were born, not of blood, nor of the will of the flesh, nor of the will of man, but of God.

And the Word was made flesh, and dwelt among us, (and we beheld his glory, the glory as of the only begotten of the Father,) full of grace and truth. . . .

And of his fulness have all we received, and grace for grace.

For the law was given by Moses, but grace and truth came by Jesus Christ.

No man hath seen God at any time ; the only begotten Son, who is in the bosom of the Father, he hath declared him.

A

THE ANNUNCIATION

St. Luke.

The angel Gabriel was sent from God unto a city of Galilee, named Nazareth,

To a virgin espoused to a man whose name was Joseph, of the house of David ; and the virgin's name was Mary.

And the angel came in unto her, and said, Hail, thou that art highly favoured, the Lord is with thee : blessed art thou among women.

And when she saw him, she was troubled at his saying, and cast in her mind what manner of salutation this should be.

And the angel said unto her, Fear not, Mary : for thou hast found favour with God.

And, behold, thou shalt conceive in thy womb, and bring forth a son, and shalt call his name JESUS.

He shall be great, and shall be called the Son of the Highest : and the Lord God shall give unto him the throne of his father David :

And he shall reign over the house of Jacob for ever ; and of his kingdom there shall be no end.

Then said Mary unto the angel, How shall this be, seeing I know not a man ?

And the angel answered and said unto her, The Holy Ghost shall come upon thee, and the power of the Highest shall overshadow thee : therefore also that holy thing which shall be born of thee shall be called the Son of God.

.   .   .   .

And Mary said, Behold the handmaid of the Lord ; be it unto me according to thy word. And the angel departed from her.

THE BIRTH OF THE VIRGIN

Fra Filippo Lippi

THE MAGNIFICAT

St. Luke.

And Mary said, My soul doth magnify the Lord,

And my spirit hath rejoiced in God my Saviour.

For he hath regarded the low estate of his handmaiden : for behold, from henceforth all generations shall call me blessed.

For he that is mighty hath done to me great things ; and holy is his name.

And his mercy is on them that fear him from generation to generation.

He hath shewed strength with his arm ; he hath scattered the proud in the imagination of their hearts.

He hath put down the mighty from their seats, and exalted them of low degree.

He hath filled the hungry with good things ; and the rich he hath sent empty away.

He hath holpen his servant Israel, in remembrance of his mercy ;

As he spake to our fathers, to Abraham, and to his seed for ever.

1

INVOCATION

Behold thy mother !—*St. John* xix. 27.

THE DIVINE LITURGY OF JAMES.

Hail, Mary, full of grace : the Lord is with thee, blessed art thou among women, and blessed is the fruit of thy womb, for thou didst bear the Saviour of our souls.

Hail in the highest, our all-holy, pure, most blessed glorious Lady, the Mother of God, and ever-Virgin Mary.

Verily it is becoming to bless thee, the Mother of God, the ever-blessed, and all-blameless, more honourable than the cherubim, and incomparably more glorious than the seraphim : thee, who didst bear with purity God the Word, thee verily the Mother of God, we magnify.

In thee, full of grace, all creation rejoices, the host of angels, and the race of men ; hallowed temple, and spiritual paradise, glory of virgins, of whom God took Flesh ; and our God, who was before the world, became a child. For He made thy womb His throne, and thy bosom broader than the heavens. In thee, O full of grace, all creation rejoices : glory unto thee.

4

ST. CYRIL OF ALEXANDRIA (Council of Ephesus, 431).

Hail, Mary, of all things in the whole world most precious. Hail, Mary, dove undefiled. Hail, Mary, inextinguishable lamp ; for of thee is born the Sun of Justice. Hail, Mary, the place of Him who is not held by place.

ST. BASIL OF SELEUCIA (329-379).

Whoso would celebrate the holy Virgin and Mother of God, will find abundant materials for praise. But I, knowing my own weakness to be unequal to the mightiness of the reality, have for a long while refrained from very awe. For I have not my lips purified with a coal from heaven, like Isaias who saw the Seraphim ; nor have I, like the divine Moses, the feet of my soul bared of their covering.

What tongue is there so eloquent as worthily to hymn her praises ? For through her name we have merited great blessings. With what flowers of eulogy shall we weave a garland befitting her ? For of her the flower of Jesse germinated, and crowned our race with glory and honour. What gifts shall we offer worthy of her, of whom all the things of this world are not worthy ? For if Paul says of the other saints, of whom the world was not worthy, what shall we say of the Mother of God, who outshines all the martyrs as much as does the sun the stars.

ST. EPHREM (Fourth Century).

My most holy Lady, Mother of God, and full of grace ; glory of our common nature ; dispenser of all good things ; after the Trinity, mistress of all ; after the Paraclete, another consoler ; and after the Mediator, the whole world's mediatress ; than cherubim and seraphim higher beyond compare, and more glorious by far ; unsearchable abyss of God's goodness; protection of the whole universe ; . . . bridge of the whole world, leading us to the heights of heaven ; key, introducing us to heaven.   O thou our patroness and mediatress, behold my confidence, and my divinely-inspired desire.

O Mother of God, greater than all thought or speech ! O Virgin, without controversy more sublime than all virginity, through whom man's nature, which, so long fallen, had departed far from God, has, by a way of inexplicable benignity and incomparable condescension, been united to the Blessed and Divine Nature.

BISHOP AEDELWALD (Ninth Century. England).

Sancta Dei genitrix semper virgo beata benedicta gloriosa et generosa, intacta et intemerata, casta et incontaminata Maria immaculata electa et a Deo dilecta ; singulari sanctitate praedita ; atque omni laude digna ; quae es interpellatrix pro totius mundi discrimine : exaudi exaudi exaudi nos sancta Maria. Ora pro nobis et intercede et auxiliari ne dedigneris.

Confidimus enim et pro certo scimus quia omne
quod vis potes impetrare a filio tuo domino nostro
Jesu Christo Deo omnipotenti omnium saeculorum
rege, qui vivit cum Patre et Spiritu Sancto in saecula
saeculorum. Amen.

TRANSLATION.

Holy Mother of God, ever Virgin ; blessed,
glorious, generous ; inviolate and without stain ;
chaste Mary immaculate, chosen and loved of God,
with singular holiness endowed, and worthy of all
praise ; who didst intervene in the whole world's
danger—Hear, O hear us, holy Mary ; pray for us
and intercede ; do not disdain to help us.

For we are confident and know for certain that
thou canst obtain by prayer all thou wilt from thy
Son, our Lord Jesus Christ, Almighty God and King
of Ages, who liveth with Father and Holy Ghost for
ever and ever. Amen.

St. Thomas of Villanova (1488-1555).

Do not labour, I pray you, to describe with charm
of fancy and eloquence of style each trait of Mary's
character. Of whatever privilege you speak, or of
whatever dignity, it is enough to have said once,
' Mary, of whom is born Jesus.' This praise is,
indeed, brief, but in its very briefness it contains all
that can be said. No, I beg of you, tarry not in
studious effort to tell in detail every perfection which

is hers. There is one word which better than a thousand books expresses what the Virgin Mother is. What, then, is that one word ? ' Mary, of whom is born Jesus.' Behold why the Gospels speak so rarely of her. That one word is quite enough. What would you wish to hear about this Most Blessed Virgin ? That she is humble, pure, full of grace, dowered with all holiness. What ? Could it be that you could conceive of her as though she were proud or impure, irritable or foolish ? Nay, rather, what gentle glory, what brilliant, what clear sweet innocence, what maiden-like reserve, what winning grace, what holy gift, can have been wanting in ' Mary, of whom is born Jesus ! ' Gaze, then, in thought upon the noblest ideal of which you can, in your fondest fancy, dream. Let your mind soar free from all fetter that would limit its flight. Set no barrier to your meditative love. Think of her, beautiful above all creatures that are of earth. Think of her, holy above all angels that are of heaven. Think of her, prudent, pure, humble, majestic, gentle, strong. Think of her, meek and lovable, as she is admirable and queenlike. You have not yet been able to express what is in that one word. She is more excellent, more perfect than your ideal. For she is ' Mary, of whom is born Jesus.'

DANTE (1265-1321).

Freely the Sage, though wrapt in musings high,
Assumed the teacher's part, and mild began. . . .

THE PRESENTATION OF THE VIRGIN

Carpaccio

'Now, raise thy view
Unto the visage most resembling Christ :
For, in her splendour only shalt thou win
The power to look on him.'
              Forthwith, I saw
Such floods of gladness on her visage showered,
From holy spirits winging that profound,
That, whatsoever I had yet beheld,
Had not so much suspended me with wonder,
Or shown me such similitude of God.
And he, who had to her descended once
On earth, now hailed in heaven; and on poised wing,
'Ave, Maria ; Gratia Plena,' sang :
To whose sweet anthem all the blissful court,
From all parts answering, rang ; that holier joy
Brooden the deep serene.
            'Father revered,
Who deignst, for me, to quit the pleasant place
Wherein thou sittest, by eternal lot,
Say, who that angel is, that with such glee
Beholds our Queen, and so enamoured glows
Of her high beauty, that all fire he seems.'

So I again resorted to the lore
Of my wise teacher, he, whom Mary's charms
Embellished, as the sun the morning star ;
Who thus in answer spake :
            'In him are summed
Whate'er of buxomness and free delight
May be in spirit, or in angel, met :
And so beseems ; for, that he bare the palm

B

Down unto Mary, when the Son of God
Vouchsafed to clothe him in terrestrial weeds.
Now, let thine eyes wait heedful on my words ;
And note thou of this just and pious realm
The chiefest nobles.   Those, highest in bliss,
The twain, on each hand next our Empress throned,
Are, as it were, two roots unto this Rose :
He to the left, the parent, whose rash taste
Proves bitter to his seed ; and, on the right,
That ancient father of the holy Church,
Into whose keeping Christ did give the keys
Of this sweet flower ; near whom, behold the Seer
That, ere he died, saw all the grievous times
Of the fair bride, who, with the lance and nails,
Was won.   And, near unto the other rests
The leader, under whom, on manna, fed
The ungrateful nation, fickle and perverse.
On the other part, facing to Peter, lo,
Where Anna sits, so well content to look
On her loved Daughter that, with moveless eye,
She chants the loud Hosanna : while, opposed
To the first father of your mortal kind,
Is Lucia, at whose hest thy lady sped,
When on the edge of ruin closed thine eye.

But (for the vision hasteneth to an end),
Here we break off, as the good workman doth,
That shapes the cloak according to the cloth ;
And to the primal love our ken shall rise
That thou may'st penetrate the brightness, far
As sight can bear thee.   Yet, alas, in sooth,

THE PRESENTATION OF THE VIRGIN

Beating thy pennons, thinking to advance,
Thou backward fallest.   Grace, then, must first be
    gained—
Her grace, whose might can help thee.   Thou in
    prayer
Seek her : and, with affection, whilst I sue,
Attend, and yield me all thy heart.'

PETRARCH'S ODE (1304-1374).

Virgin most Fair, who, clad and crown'd with sun
    And stars, didst please the Sun supreme so well,
        That for his light he made a tent in thee,
    Love bids me something of thy praises tell,
But nought, without thy aid, can be begun,
        And his, who loved thy body's guest to be.
        I cry to one, who answers graciously
Whoe'er in faith implore.
If ever yet the sore
        Sufferings of man have touch'd thy clemency,
Virgin, oh, now to my petition lean ;
        Do thou my warfare aid,
        Though I be made
Of earth, and thou Heaven's Queen.
        .   .   .   .   .   .

Virgin most Pure, in whom no blemish lies,
    Daughter and Mother of thy Birth Divine,
        Light of this life, of yonder life the Grace,
Thou bright and lofty Window of the skies,
    By thee our most High Father's Child and thine
        Came down to save the latest of our race ;
        And, amid every mortal dwelling-place,

Thou, Saintly Maid, alone
Wast chosen, that the moan
    Of Eve thou shouldst with jubilee replace.
Oh, make me, for thou canst, His grace beseem,
    Thou that beyond all bound
    Art blest, and crowned
In yonder court supreme.

Virgin most Holy, full of grace, that wast
    Exalted by thy deep, true humbleness
        To heav'n, whence thou my orison dost hear ;
    Thou broughtest forth the Fount of tenderness
And Sun of justice, who the world, when lost
        In errors dense and dark, made bright and clear.
        Three names thou linkest, that are sweet and
        dear—
Mother and Child and Bride.
O Virgin glorified
    Queen of that Lord who, to this earthly sphere,
Loosing our bonds, brought liberty with bliss ;
    True Comforter, impart
    Peace to my heart
By those blest wounds of His.

    .   .   .   .   .   .

Virgin Humane, pride's Foe, if dear thou hold
    The common prototype of thee and us,
        Have pity upon my humbled heart contrite.
    For, if I loved, with faith so marvellous,
A piece of earth, a brittle mortal mould,
        Thou, noblest thing, may'st more my zeal incite.
        If then, from my debased and wretched plight,

Thy hand uplifteth me,
Virgin, I pledge to thee
    My chastened pen, my thoughts, my inmost might,
My tongue, my heart, and every tear and sigh ;
    Oh, let my changed desire
    Thy grace acquire;
Guide me where true fords lie.

CHAUCER (1340-1400).

O Lord, our Lord, how wondrously (quoth she)
    Thy name in this large world is spread abroad ;
For not alone by men of dignity
    Thy worship is performed and precious laud ;
But, by the mouths of children, gracious God,
Thy goodness is set forth ; they, when they lie
Upon the breast, thy name do glorify.

Wherefore in praise, the worthiest that I may,
    Jesu, of thee, and the white Lily-flower
Which did Thee bear, and is a Maid for aye,
    To tell a story I will use my power ;
Not that I may increase her honour's dower,
For she herself is Honour, and the Root
Of goodness, next her Son, our soul's best boot.

O Mother-Maid, O Maid and Mother free,
    O Bush unburnt, burning in Moses' sight,
That down didst ravish from the Deity,
    Through humbleness, the Spirit that did alight
Upon thy heart, whence, through that glory's might,
Conceivèd was the Father's Sapience—
Help me to tell it in thy reverence.

Lady, thy goodness, thy magnificence,
  Thy virtue and thy great humility,
Surpass all science and all utterance ;
  For sometimes, Lady, ere men pray to thee,
Thou goest before in thy benignity,
The light to us vouchsafing of thy prayer,
To be our guide unto thy Son so dear.

My knowledge is so weak, O blissful Queen,
  To tell abroad thy mighty worthiness,
That I the weight of it may not sustain ;
  But, as a child of twelve months old, or less,
That laboureth his language to express,
Even so fare I ; and therefore, I thee pray,
Guide thou my song which I of thee shall say.

HENRY A. RAWES (1826-1885).

Blest Mother of my Lord, I fly to thee,
Who ever hast a mother's love for me,
Who prayest ceaselessly to God for me.

Thou Queen, who givest gifts of light to me,
In joy and weariness I turn to thee,
Lifting my hands and all my heart to thee.

No love of Jesus is flame-winged like thine,
For all His overflowing Heart is thine ;
My Mother Mary, make thy Jesus mine.

THE EDUCATION OF THE VIRGIN
Murillo

No heart is steeped in love of God like thine ;
No spirit lightens in His eyes like thine ;
Thou loving Mother, make thy Jesus mine.

I seek, and cannot find Him without thee ;
Or worship Him, or love Him without thee ;
For He is thine, and evermore with thee.

But always do I find my Love with thee ;
For thou didst bring my dearest Love to me ;
Oh, bring Him now ; oh, bring thy Son to me.

Thou chosen Daughter of the Living One ;
Thou sun-clothed Mother of the Living One ;
Thou Bride, star-crownèd, of the Living One ;

.   .   .   .   .   .

Thou helpest souls on earth who know not thee,
The souls who trust with childlike love to thee,
The souls who look in pain and grief to thee.

Help thou all suffering souls, most loving One ;
Much solace give to them, most loving One ;
Remembering thine own pain, most loving One.

A flower-like splendour in the love of God,
Thy soul most filled with sweetest bliss of God,
Thou liest crowned upon the Heart of God.

My Mother, thou art dearest to the King,
Touching the golden sceptre of the King,
Thy sinless hands uplifting to the King.

My Mother, evermore the Queen of Heaven,
The risen stars are round thy throne in heaven ;
Thy Son, the Saint's Desire, is King of Heaven.

Bring me in safety where I wish to be,
To light of promise, where I pray to be,
The heaven of Jesus, where I long to be.

Bring me to Him who sought on earth for me—
Who lived, divinely sorrowful, for me—
Thy Jesus, Son of God, who died for me.

F. W. FABER (1814-1863).

But scornful men have coldly said,
    Thy love was leading me from God ;
And yet in this I did but tread
    The very path my Saviour trod.

They know but little of thy worth,
    Who speak these heartless words to me ;
For what did Jesus love on earth
    One half so tenderly as thee ?

PRAYER OF ST. ANSELM (1033-1109. Archbishop
    of Canterbury).

Of a certainty, O Jesus, Son of God, and thou, O
Mother Mary, you desire that whatever you love
should be loved by us. Therefore, O good Son, I
beg Thee, by the love Thou bearest Thy Mother, and

THE MARRIAGE OF THE VIRGIN

Raphael

as Thou wishest her to be loved, to grant to me that
I may truly love her. And thou, O good Mother, I
beg thee by the love thou bearest thy Son, as thou
wishest Him to be loved, to pray for me that I may
truly love Him. Behold I ask nothing that is not
in accordance with your will. Since, then, this is in
your power, shall my sins prevent its being done?
O Jesus, lover of men, Thou wert able to love criminals
even so as to die for them ; canst Thou, then, refuse
me, who ask only the love of Thee and Thy Mother?
And thou, too, Mary, Mother of Him who loved us,
who didst bear Him in thy womb, and feed Him at
thy breast, art thou not able, or not willing, to obtain
for one who asks it the love of thy Son and of thyself?

Oh, may then my mind venerate you both as you
deserve ! may my heart love you, as it is right it should !
may my body serve you, as it ought ! in your service
may my life be spent ! and may my whole substance
praise you in eternity ! Blessed be God for ever.
Amen, amen.

The Roman Breviary.

> Hail, O Queen of Heav'n enthron'd !
> Hail, by Angels mistress own'd,
> Root of Jesse, gate of morn,
> Whence the world's true Light was born.
> Glorious Virgin, joy to thee,
> Loveliest whom in heaven they see !
> Fairest thou where all are fair !
> Plead with Christ our sins to spare.

c

THE ANNUNCIATION

The Holy Ghost shall come upon thee, and the power of the Highest
shall overshadow thee : therefore also that holy thing which shall be
born of thee shall be called the Son of God.—*St. Luke* i. 35.

ROBERT STEPHEN HAWKER (1803-1875).

A shape, like folded light, embodied air,
    Yet wreathed with flesh, and warm :
All that of heaven is feminine and fair,
    Moulded in visible form,

She stood, the Lady Shechinah of earth,
    A chancel for the sky :
Where woke, to breath and beauty, God's own
        Birth,
    For man to see Him by.

Round her, too pure to mingle with the day,
    Light, that as life, abode ;
Folded within her fibres meekly lay
    The link of boundless God.

So linked, so blent, that when, with pulse fulfilled,
    Moved by that Infant Hand,
Far, far away, His conscious Godhead thrilled,
    And stars might understand.

Lo ! where they pause, with inter-gathering rest,
    The Threefold, and the One ;

THE ANNUNCIATION

Donatello

And lo, He binds them to her orient breast,
His manhood girded on.

The zone, where two glad worlds for ever meet,
Beneath that bosom ran :
Deep in that womb the conquering Paraclete
Smote Godhead on to man.

Sole scene among the stars, where, yearning, glide
The Threefold and the One ;
Her God upon her lap, the Virgin Bride,
Her awful Child, her Son !

CHRISTOPHER HARVEY (1597-1663).
Unto the music of the spheres
Let men, and Angels, join in concert theirs.
So great a messenger
From heaven to earth
Is seldom seen,
Attired in so much glory :
A message welcomer,
Fraught with more mirth,
Hath never been
Subject of any story :
This by a double right, if any, may
Be truly styled the world's birth-day.

The making of the world ne'er cost
So dear, by much, as to redeem it lost.
God said but, *Let it be*,
And every thing
Was made straightway,
So as he saw it good :

But ere that he could see
A course to bring
Man gone astray
To the place where he stood,
His wisdom with his mercy, for man's sake,
Against his justice part did take.

And the result was this day's news,
Able the messenger himself t'amuse,
As well as her, to whom
By him 'twas told,
That though she were
A Virgin pure, and knew
No man, yet in her womb
A son she should
Conceive and bear,
As sure as God was true.
Such high place in his favour she possess'd,
Being among all women bless'd.

But bless'd especially in this,
That she believed, and for eternal bliss
Relied on him, whom she
Herself should bear,
And her own son
Took for her Saviour.
And if there any be,
That when they hear,
As she had done,
Suit their behaviour,
They may be blessèd, as she was, and say,
'Tis their Annunciation-day.

FELICIA D. HEMANS (1793-1835).

Lowliest of Women, and most glorified :
In thy still beauty, sitting calm and lone :
A brightness round thee grew ; and by thy side,
Kindling the air, a Form ethereal shone,
Solemn, yet breathing gladness.   From her throne
A Queen had risen with more imperial eye ;
A stately Prophetess of victory
From her proud lyre had struck a tempest's tone.
For such high tidings as to thee were brought,
    Chosen of heaven, that hour : but thou, O thou,
E'en as a flower with gracious rains o'erfraught,
    Thy Virgin-head beneath its crown didst bow,
And take to thy meek breast the All-holy Word,
And own thyself the Handmaid of the Lord.

LAURENCE HOUSMAN (1865-).

A Garden bower in bower
Grew waiting for God's hour :
Where no man ever trod,
This was the Gate of God.

The first bower was red—
Her lips which ' welcome ' said.
The second bower was blue—
Her eyes that let God through.

The third bower was white—
Her soul as in God's sight.
Three bowers of love
Won Christ from Heaven above.

JOHN DONNE (1573-1631).

Salvation to all that will is nigh :
　　That All which always is All everywhere ;
　　Which cannot sin, and yet, all sins must bear ;
Which cannot die, yet, cannot choose but die—
Lo, faithful Virgin, yields Himself to lie
　　In prison in thy womb ; and though He there
　　Can take no sin, nor thou give, yet He 'll wear,
Taken from thence, flesh which death's force may
　　　　try.
Ere by the spheres time was created, thou
　　Wast in His mind—which is thy Son and Brother,
　　Whom thou conceivedst—conceived ; yea, thou
　　　　art now
Thy Maker's Maker, and thy Father's Mother ;
　　Thou hast Light in dark, and shut in little room,
Immensity, cloistered in thy dear womb.

F. W. H. MYERS (1843-1901).

Yes, and to her, the Beautiful and Lowly,
　　Mary a Maiden, separate from men,
Camest Thou nigh and didst possess her wholly,
　　Close to Thy Saints, but Thou wast closer then.

Once and for ever didst Thou show Thy Chosen,
　　Once and for ever magnify Thy choice—
Scorched in love's fire, or with his freezing frozen,
　　Lift up your hearts, ye humble, and rejoice.

THE ANNUNCIATION

Botticelli

Not to the rich He came and to the ruling—
  Men full of meat, whom wholly He abhors—
Not to the fools grown insolent in fooling
  Most, when the lost are dying at the doors.

Nay, but to her who with a sweet thanksgiving
  Took in tranquillity what God might bring,
Blessed Him and waited, and within her living
  Felt the arousal of a Holy Thing.

Aye, for her infinite and endless honour
  Found the Almighty in this flesh a tomb,
Pouring with power the Holy Ghost upon her,
  Nothing disdainful of the Virgin's womb.

JEAN BAPTISTE DE SANTEUIL (1630-1697).

Oh, joyful was the morn
That told of peace and love
To man, the ruined and forlorn,
Descending from above.
Though far from Eden's bowers,
By sad transgression driven,
A lovelier Eden shall be ours—
  For Christ came down from heaven.
From God's eternal breast
He stooped to time and space,
And found with thee, O Maiden blest,
  His lowly dwelling-place.
And lowlier, in the tomb,
He scornèd not to lie,

That our frail mortal might assume
His immortality.

An angel from beyond the clouds
The awful mystery unshrouds,
Announcing that the time hath come,
And God doth fill the Virgin's womb.
Oh, blest above all power to tell
Is she in whom the Lord doth dwell,
Who, bearing such an heavenly load,
Becomes the Mother of our God.
A Virgin pure she needs must be
To give that flesh from all sin free ;
And with the Holy Ghost combined,
To form the Saviour of mankind.
The world's Creator, for our sakes,
From Mary's breast his nurture takes ;
That he, who is the angels' food,
May feed us with his Flesh and Blood.

F. W. FABER (1814-1863).

Like the dawning of the morning
  On the mountain's golden heights ;
Like the breaking of the moonbeams
  On the gloom of cloudy nights ;
Like a secret told by angels,
  Getting known upon the earth—
Is the Mother's expectation
  Of Messias' speedy birth.

THE ANNUNCIATION

Gentileschi

Thou wert happy, blessèd Mother,
  With the very bliss of heaven,
Since the angel's salutation
  In thy raptured ear was given ;
Since the Ave of that midnight,
  When thou wert anointed Queen,
Like a river overflowing
  Hath the grace within thee been.

On the mountains of Judea,
  Like the chariot of the Lord,
Thou wert lifted in thy spirit
  By the Uncreated Word ;
Gifts and graces flowed upon thee
  In a sweet celestial strife,
And the growing of thy Burden
  Was the lightening of thy life.

.   .   .   .

Every moment did that Burden
  Press upon thee with new grace ;
Happy Mother, thou art longing
  To behold the Saviour's face :
Oh, his human face and features
  Must be passing sweet to see ;
Thou hast seen them, happy Mother,
  Ah then, show them now to me.

AUBREY THOMAS DE VERE (1814-1902).

The crown of creatures, first in place,
  Was, of all creatures, creature most :

D

By nature nothing : all by grace ;
   Redemption's first and loftiest boast.

Handmaid of God in heart and will,
   Without His life she seemed a death,
A void that He alone could fill,
   A word suspended on His breath.

Yet—void and nothing—she in Him
   The creature's sole perfection found ;
She was the great Rock's shadow dim ;
   She was the silence not the sound.

On golden airs, by Him upheld,
   She knelt, a soft Subjection mute,
A hushed Dependence, tranced and spelled,
   Still yearning towards the Absolute.

She was a sea-shell from the deep
   Of God ; her function this alone
Of Him to whisper as in sleep,
   In everlasting undertone.

This hour on Him her eyes are set !
   And those who tread the earth she trod
Like her themselves in her forget,
   And her remember but in God.

ADELAIDE A. PROCTER (1825-1864).

    Be still, ye clouds of Heaven !
    Be silent, Earth !
    And hear an Angel tell
    Of Jesus' birth.

.   .   .   .

THE VISITATION

Andrea della Robbia

Be still—Pride, War and Pomp,
  Vain Hopes, vain Fears,
For now an Angel speaks,
  And Mary hears.

' Hail, Mary ! ' lo, it rings
  Through ages on ;
' Hail, Mary,' it shall sound,
  Till time is done.

' Hail, Mary ! ' infant lips
  Lisp it to-day ;
' Hail, Mary ! ' with faint smile
  The dying say ;

' Hail, Mary ! ' many a heart
  Broken with grief,
In that angelic prayer
  Has found relief.

And many a half-lost soul
  When turned at bay
With those triumphant words
  Has won the day.

THE ROMAN BREVIARY.

Mother of Christ ! hear thou thy people's cry.
Star of the deep, and portal of the sky !
Mother of Him who thee from nothing made,
Sinking we strive, and call to thee for aid :
Oh, by that joy which Gabriel brought to thee,
Thou Virgin first and last, let us thy mercy see.

III

THE NATIVITY

And there were in the same country shepherds abiding in the field,
keeping watch over their flock by night. And, lo, the angel of the
Lord came upon them, and the glory of the Lord shone round about
them: and they were sore afraid. And the angel said unto them,
Fear not: for, behold, I bring you good tidings of great joy, which
shall be to all people. For unto you is born this day in the city of
David a Saviour, which is Christ the Lord. And this shall be a
sign unto you; Ye shall find the babe wrapped in swaddling clothes,
lying in a manger. And suddenly there was with the angel a
multitude of the heavenly host praising God, and saying, Glory to
God in the highest, and on earth peace, good will toward men.—
St. Luke ii. 8-14.

CANTICLE OF ST. EPHREM (Fourth Century).

When the Son was born, light shone forth, darkness was chased away from earth, and the world was
illumined. Let it, therefore, praise the Son, the
Splendour of the Father, who illumined it. . . .

The blaze of His light went through the East; a
star lit up Persia; the rising of Christ allured her, and
announced to her that the Victim was come which
moves all to rejoice.

Great Assyria, well-instructed, called the Magi,
saying: 'Take presents and go to Judæa, to honour
the King there born.'

The princes of Persia with exultation took presents

28

from their country, and brought to the Son of the Virgin gold, myrrh, and frankincense.

Entering the house of the poor little Maid, they found therein the Infant lying ; and drawing nigh to Him, they adored with exultation, and opened their treasures before Him.

Thereat said Mary : ' For whom are these ? For what cause ? And what may be the reason that has called you from your country, that ye should come with your treasures to the Child ? ' . . .

They make answer : ' Thy Son is a King ; and on His head are gathered all diadems in one, since of all is He king : His power is more high than the world, and His empire all things obey.

' A great treasure is thy Son : His riches suffice to make all rich. Treasures of kings will sometimes fail, but He can neither fail, nor be ever measured.' . . .

' Ye men, you must inquire who the King is, before you adore Him, lest you should perchance have gone a wrong way, and some other be the new-born King.

' He is but a little tiny infant ; and lo, as you may see, He has neither royal diadem, nor throne. What have you then seen to make you pour forth your treasures, and honour Him as King ? '

' A little one He is because Himself has so willed ; and He loves meekness and humility until He is made manifest. But the time will be, when before Him all diadems shall bow down, and shall adore Him.' . . .

' My Son has neither armies, nor legions, nor troops; He is lying in His Mother's poverty. Why do you call Him King ? '

'Heavenly are the armies of thy Son ; in the firmament do they move ; everywhere do they spread abroad their glittering rays : from amongst them one has come to call us. Our whole country was in alarm.'

'Quite recent is the infant. How then should He be a King, since to the world He is unknown ? How could this little one reign over men powerful and renowned ? ' . . .

'Old is thy little one, O Virgin. He is the Ancient of days, and before all times. Adam is much His junior. By Him shall all things be renewed.'

'Surely it behoves you to expose the whole mystery; and explain who revealed to you the mystery of my Son, who in your parts is a King.'

'A great star appeared to us, more splendid than all the other stars. With its light our land was lit up. It gave to us the news that a King was born.'

'I should be loath that you tell this story in our country, lest the kings of our land from envy lay snares for the Infant.'

'Fear not, O Virgin ; for thy Son will bring to nought all diadems, and tread them under foot ; nor by their envy will the kings have power to hurt Him.'

'I fear Herod, that unclean fox, lest he perturb me, and, drawing his sword, cut off the sweet cluster whilst yet unripe.'

'From Herod fear nought, because by thy Son it is that his throne subsists. For as soon as thy Son shall have begun to reign, Herod's throne will be destroyed, and his crown will fall to the ground.'

'A very torrent of blood is Jerusalem : in it all the

THE VISITATION

Albertinelli

best men are being slaughtered : if he should have his attention drawn to the Infant, he will fall on Him. Therefore speak secretly, and act without noise.'

'All the torrents and swords shall be laid at rest through thy Son. Blunted is the sword of Jerusalem, and refuses to serve for slaughterers.'

'The scribes and priests of Jerusalem help on the shedding of blood, and are void of understanding : deadly strife will they stir up against me, and against the Child. Magi, I beg you, keep silence. . . .

'The Angel revealed to me when I conceived, that my Son would be King, and signified to me, as he has done to you, that His crown is from on high and can never be broken. . . .

'The Angel who appeared to me explained at the Annunciation that His Kingdom would have no end ; but that the secret must be kept, and not be made known.' . . .

'From out of the entire heaven one single star has stirred together Persia, which is certified that thy Son is the Son of God, and that to Him all nations will be made subject.'

'May Persia rejoice at your tidings ; may Assyria exult at your return ; and when the reign of my Son shall arise, Himself will plant His standard in your country.

'Let the Church sing out with gladness : Glory to the Son of the Most High by whom the heights and the depths are illumined. Blessed is He who by His birth has made all things joyful.'

ADESTE, FIDELES (Seventeenth Century).

Come hither, ye faithful,
Joyful and triumphant,
Come hither, come hither, run Bethlehemward ;
See who is born here ;
'Tis the King of Angels :
Come, let us all adore Him,
Come, let us all adore Him,
Come, let us all adore Him, Christ our Lord.

Godhead of Godhead,
Light of Light Eternal,
Birth doth a Maiden Him accord ;
True God, made not,
But indeed begotten :
Come, let us all adore Him,

The shepherds now hasten
To the lowly stable,
Allowed to abandon their watch and ward :
Let us, rejoicing,
Hurry on as they do :
Come, let us all adore Him,

Then the star-led Magi,
Christ in turn adoring,
Gold, myrrh, and incense to Him award ;
Giving our hearts thus
To the new-born Jesus,
Come, let us all adore Him,

THE NATIVITY

Nicolo Pisano

The Light co-eternal,
Son of God the Father,
Veiled in our flesh will our eyes reward :
God, as an infant
Swathed in bands and swaddled,
Come, let us all adore Him,

For Him, who for our sakes
Was poor in the manger,
Let our love's embraces some warmth afford :
Who would not love Him
Who so much have loved us ?
Come, let us all adore Him,

Sing Alleluias,
All ye choirs of Angels ;
Sound now, ye Blessèd, your sweetest chord :
Glory, be glory
Unto God in Heaven.
Come, let us all adore Him,

Then, to Thee, Jesus,
Glory be for ever,
Born when the midnight turned morningward :
Word of the Father,
Now for us incarnate,
Come, let us all adore Him,
Come, let us all adore Him,
Come, let us all adore Him, Christ our Lord.

MILTON (1608-1674).

　　　It was the winter wild,
　　　While the heaven-born child
All meanly wrapt in the rude manger lies ;
　　　Nature in awe to Him
　　　Had doffed her gaudy trim,
With her great Master so to sympathize.
　　　It was no season then for her
　　　To wanton with the Sun her lusty paramour.

　　.　　　.　　　.　　　.　　.

　　　No war or battle's sound
　　　Was heard the world around ;
The idle spear and shield were high up hung ;
　　　The hookèd chariot stood,
　　　Unstained with hostile blood ;
The trumpet spake not to the armèd throng ;
　　　And kings sat still with awful eye,
　　　As if they surely knew their sovran Lord was by.

　　.　　.　　.　　.　　.

　　　The shepherds on the lawn,
　　　Or ere the point of dawn,
Sat simply chatting in a rustic row ;
　　　Full little thought they than
　　　That the mighty Pan
Was kindly come to live with them below.
　　　Perhaps their loves, or else their sheep,
　　　Was all that did their silly thoughts so busy keep.

　　.　　.　　.　　.　　.

　　　At last surrounds their sight
　　　A globe of circular light,

THE NATIVITY

Piero della Francesca

That with long beams the shame-faced Night arrayed.
    The helmed Cherubim,
    And sworded Seraphim,
Are seen, in glittering ranks with wings displayed,
    Harping, in loud and solemn quire,
    With unexpressive notes to Heaven's new-born
      Heir.

    Such music—as 'tis said—
    Before was never made,
But when of old the Sons of Morning sung ;
    While the Creator great
    His constellations set,
And the well-balanced World on hinges hung,
    And cast the dark foundations deep,
    And bid the weltering waves their oozy channel
      keep.

JACOPONE DA TODI (1228-1306).

    Full of joy His beauteous Mother
    Stood beside our new-born Brother,
      Who was cradled in the hay ;
    And her spirit's exultation
    Thrilled her frame with sweet elation,
      To behold Him where He lay.

    Oh ! what deep, ecstatic feeling,
    O'er the stainless Mother stealing,
      Marked the Sole-Begotten's birth :

How her soul's own silent laughter
Filled her gaze the moment after
    She first saw His face on earth.

Whose the eyes that would not measure,
Wonder-wide, that Mother's pleasure,
    Like to which no bliss hath been :
His in sooth were utmost rapture
Who one glimpse of her could capture,
    At her mother-play serene.

Christ she saw, in wintry weather,
Housed with ox and ass together,
    For His sinful human race :
Saw His creatures bend before Him—
Wailful Sweeting !—to adore Him,
    In His lowly lodging-place.

Compassing the crib completely,
Angels many sang full sweetly
    Their immeasurable joy ;
Where an old man with the Maiden
Silent stood, their hearts o'erladen
    Wondering o'er her wondrous Boy.

Fount of Love, my Mother Mary !
Yield me love, nor let me vary
    In this love that flows from thee :
Let me love my God and Saviour
So, that with my heart's behaviour
    Even His well pleased may be.

Mother mine ! this favour do me :
Let His pain, gone through and through me,
    Rest implanted in my heart :
Of the pangs that in the manger
Lay for earth's celestial Stranger
    Let me bear, like thee, my part.

Make me joy with thee more truly,
To thy little Jesus duly
    Clinging till my life be past ;
Yield me of thy Babe fruition,
And my exile's one ambition
    Be, like thine, to hold Him fast :
Spread throughout the world such longing,
And, when souls to Him come thronging,
    Let mine be at least the last.

Virgin of all virgins, take me
Into grace again, and make me
    Catch thy Baby to my breast :
Let me bear thy beauteous Burden,
Born that, life's immortal guerdon,
    Dying, He from death should wrest.

Let my heart, like thine, be sated
With Him, nay, inebriated,
    Dancing in its mystic bliss :
Overcome are all my senses
With a wonder that immense is,
    At communion such as this.

Keep me, under thy protection,
For thy Son, from all defection
    Warded by His word, His grace :
When my dust to dust returneth,
That for which my spirit yearneth
    Grant me, too—to see His face.

JOHN KEBLE (1792-1866).

Ave Maria ! Blessèd Maid !
Lily of Eden's fragrant shade,
    Who can express the love
That nurtured thee, so pure and sweet,
Making thy heart a shelter meet
    For Jesus' holy dove !

Ave Maria ! Mother blest
To whom, caressing and caressed,
    Clings the eternal Child ;
Favoured beyond archangel's dream
When first on thee with tenderest gleam
    The new-born Saviour smiled.

Thou wept'st, meek Maiden, Mother mild,
Thou wept'st upon thy sinless Child,
    Thy very heart was riven ;
And yet, what mourning matron here
Would deem thy sorrows bought too dear
    By all on this side heaven !

THE NATIVITY

Geertgen tot Sint Jans

A Son that never did amiss,
That never shamed His Mother's kiss,
    Nor crossed her fondest prayer ;
E'en from the Tree He deigned to bow
For her His agonizèd brow,
    Her, His sole earthly care.

Ave Maria ! thou whose name
All but adoring love may claim,
    Yet may we reach thy shrine ;
For He, thy Son and Saviour, vows
To crown all lofty lowly brows
    With love and joy like thine.

CHRISTOPHER HARVEY (1597-1663).

Unfold thy face, unmaske thy ray,
Shine forth, bright Sunne, double the day.
Let no malignant misty fume,
Nor foggy vapour, once presume
To interpose thy perfect sight
This day, which makes us love thy light
For ever better, that we could
That blessèd object once behold,
Which is both the circumference,
And center of all excellence :
Or rather neither, but a treasure
Unconfinèd without measure,
Whose center and circumference,
Including all preheminence,

Excluding nothing but defect,
And infinite in each respect,
Is equally both here and there,
And now and then and every where,
And alwaies, one, himselfe, the same,
A beeing farre above a name.
Draw neer then, and freely poure
Forth all thy light into that houre,
Which was crownèd with his birth,
And made heaven envy earth.
     Let not his birth-day clouded be,
     By whom thou shinest, and we see.

RICHARD CRASHAW (? 1613-1649).

Gloomy night embraced the place
   Where the noble Infant lay,
The Babe looked up and showed His face—
   In spite of darkness it was day !
It was Thy day, Sweet, and did rise,
   Not from the East, but from Thine eyes.

We saw Thee in Thy balmy nest,
   Bright dawn of our eternal day ;
We saw Thine eyes break from the East,
   And chase the trembling shades away ;
We saw Thee (and we blessed the sight),
   We saw Thee by Thy own sweet light.

Welcome to our wondering sight,
   Eternity shut in a span !

Summer in winter ! Day in night !
  Heaven in earth ! and God in man !
Great little One, whose glorious birth
  Lifts earth to Heaven, stoops Heaven to earth.

A CAROL OF THE TIME OF HENRY VI.

  I sing of a Maiden
    That is makeless ;
  King of all Kings
    To her Son she chess.
  He came also still,
    There his Mother was,
  As dew in April
    That falleth on the grass.
  He came also still
    To his Mother's bower,
  As dew in April
    That falleth on the flower.
  He came also still,
    There his Mother lay,
  As dew in April
    That falleth on the spray.
  Mother and Maiden
    Was never none but she ;
  Well may such a Lady
    God's Mother be.

F

CHRISTINA ROSSETTI (1830-1894).

In the bleak mid-winter
    Frosty wind made moan,
Earth stood hard as iron,
    Water like a stone ;
Snow had fallen, snow on snow,
    Snow on snow,
In the bleak mid-winter
    Long ago.

Our God, heaven cannot hold Him,
    Nor earth sustain :
Heaven and earth shall flee away
    When He comes to reign :
In the bleak mid-winter
    A stable-place sufficed
The Lord God Almighty
    Jesus Christ.

Enough for Him Whom cherubim
    Worship night and day,
A breastful of milk
    And a manger full of hay ;
Enough for Him Whom angels
    Fall down before,
The ox and ass and camel
    Which adore.

Angels and archangels
    May have gathered there,
Cherubim and seraphim
    Thronged the air,

THE NATIVITY

Botticelli

But only His mother
In her maiden bliss
Worshipped the Belovèd
With a kiss.

DANTE GABRIEL ROSSETTI (1828-1882).

This is that blessed Mary, pre-elect
God's Virgin.   Gone is a great while, and she
Dwelt young in Nazareth of Galilee.
Unto God's will she brought devout respect,
Profound simplicity of intellect,
And supreme patience.   From her mother's knee
Faithful and hopeful ; wise in charity ;
Strong in grave peace ; in pity circumspect.
So held she through her girlhood ; as it were
An angel-watered lily, that near God
Grows and is quiet.   Till, one dawn at home
She woke in her white bed and had no fear
At all, yet wept till sunshine, and felt awed
Because the fullness of the time was come.

ST. JOHN CHRYSOSTOM (347-407).

As an artist when he has found some very service-
able material fashions it into a most beautiful vessel,
so Christ, on finding the holy body and soul of the
Virgin, constructed for Himself a living temple, and
formed, in the way He willed, man in the Virgin, and,
having clothed Himself therewith, came forth to-day.
But what do I say, or how shall I speak ?   For the
marvel astounds me.   The Ancient of days has
become an infant.   He who is seated on His high and

lofty throne is laid in a manger. The impalpable, simple, incomposite, and incorporeal, is swayed about in human hands. He who bursts asunder the chains of sin is folded in swathing-bands ; since thus He wills it. For He wills to make dishonour, honour ; to clothe the inglorious with glory, and to show forth the very limit of contumely as the measure of virtue. Hence He bears with my body, that I may have room for His Word ; and taking my flesh He gives me His own Spirit, that by this giving and taking He may bestow on me the treasure of life. He takes my flesh that He may sanctify me, He gives me His Spirit that He may save me.

Robert Hugh Benson (1871-1914).

There went a merry company
    On the road to Bethlehem,
Going all to taxèd be
By the governour's decree
    On the road to Bethlehem—
Would I had been there to see.
Would I had been there to see
    On the road to Bethlehem ;
Mary, Joseph, pray for me !

Coldly blew the wind and snow
    On the road to Bethlehem.
Two there were that walkèd slow
All that day so long ago,
    On the road to Bethlehem ;
Would I had been there also.

Would I had been there to see
    On the road to Bethlehem ;
Mary, Joseph, pray for me !

One, a maid of high degree,
    On the road to Bethlehem,
Walking, walking, wearily ;—
' Joseph—Joseph, wait for me
    On the road to Bethlehem ! '
Would I had been there to see.
Would I had been there to see
    On the road to Bethlehem ;
Mary, Joseph, pray for me !

Thus they came the town within
    To the town of Bethlehem ;
Sought they straight the public inn,
So they might a shelter win
    In the town of Bethlehem ;
See them tirling at the pin.
Would I had been there to see
    On the road to Bethlehem ;
Mary, Joseph, pray for me.

' Get you gone—the night is late
    In the town of Bethlehem.'
Hear them chapping at the gate,
Richer folk both small and great,
    In the town of Bethlehem—
When they knock the poor must wait.

Would I had been there to see
On the road to Bethlehem ;
Mary, Joseph, pray for me !

Sought they straight the stable door
In the town of Bethlehem.
Mary dropped upon the floor ;
Wearied was she—wearied sore
In the town of Bethlehem.
' Joseph dear—I can no more.'
Would I had been there to see
On the road to Bethlehem ;
Mary, Joseph, pray for me !

' Cheer thee, cheer thee, Mary Maid,
In the town of Bethlehem—
See the straw is smoothly laid.'
Poor folks' wages, poorly paid,
In the town of Bethlehem !
Would I had been there to aid.
Would I had been there to see
On the road to Bethlehem ;
Mary, Joseph, pray for me !

What a lodging, cold and bare,
In the town of Bethlehem.
Bring me wrappings fine and fair,
Silk and satin rich and rare,
In the town of Bethlehem—
Lay our Lady softly there !

THE NATIVITY

Correggio

Would I had been there to see
　　On the road to Bethlehem ;
Mary, Joseph, pray for me !

Nay, no silk or satin bright
　　In the town of Bethlehem !
Think ye on this wondrous sight
Soon to see : The Lord of Light
　　In the town of Bethlehem
Comes in lowliness to-night.
Would I had been there to see
　　On the road to Bethlehem ;
Mary, Joseph, pray for me !

Ox and ass with patient pace,
　　In the town of Bethlehem,
Mark the Maiden full of grace
Lying by the manger-place
　　In the town of Bethlehem—
Lying in such sorry case.
Would I had been there to see
　　On the road to Bethlehem ;
Mary, Joseph, pray for me !

Ere the night had passed to morn,
　　In the town of Bethlehem,
Rose the Sun on us forlorn ;
In the manger old and worn,
　　In the town of Bethlehem,
Jesus Christ our Lord was born.

Would I had been there to see
    On the road to Bethlehem ;
Mary, Joseph, pray for me !

Eastern Kings are on their way
    To the town of Bethlehem ;
Shepherds run ere break of day
At His Feet their vows to pay
    In the town of Bethlehem,
Where a God Incarnate lay.
Would I had been there to see
    On the road to Bethlehem ;
Mary, Joseph, pray for me !

Christian souls, with one accord
    Come to Holy Bethlehem ;
Meet Him at His Holy Board ;
Praise the Saviour, praise the Lord,—
    In the town of Bethlehem
Who on us His glory poured !
Would I had been there to see
    In the town of Bethlehem ;
Mary, Joseph, pray for me !

THE ADORATION OF THE MAGI

Orcagna

IV

MADONNA'S LULLABY

St. Alphonsus Maria de Liguori (1696-1787).
    Mary sings : the ravished heavens
        Hush the music of their spheres ;
    Soft her voice, her beauty fairer
        Than the glancing stars appears :
            While to Jesus, slumbering nigh,
            Thus she sings her lullaby :

    ' Sleep, my Babe, my God, my Treasure,
        Gently sleep : but ah, the sight
    With its beauty so transports me,
        I am dying of delight :
            Thou canst not thy Mother see,
            Yet thou breathest flames to me.

    ' If within your lids unfolded,
        Slumbering eyes, you seem so fair ;
    When upon my gaze you open,
        How shall I your beauty bear ?
            Ah, I tremble when you wake,
            Lest my heart with love should break.

    ' Cheeks, than sweetest roses sweeter,
        Mouth, where lurks a smile divine—
                        G

Though the kiss my Babe should waken,
   I must press those lips to mine :
     Pardon, Dearest, if I say—
     Mother's love will take no Nay.'

As she ceased, the gentle Virgin
   Clasped the Infant to her breast ;
And upon his radiant forehead
   Many a loving kiss impressed :
     Jesus woke, and on her face
     Fixed a look of heavenly grace.

Ah, that look, those eyes, that beauty,
   How they pierce the Mother's heart ;
Shafts of love from every feature
   Through her gentle bosom dart :
     Heart of stone—can I behold
     Mary's love, and still be cold ?

Where, my soul, thy sense, thy reason ?
   When will these delays be o'er ?
All things else, how fair so ever,
   Are but smoke : resist no more.
     Yes, 'tis done : I yield my arms
     Captive to those double charms.

If alas, O heavenly Beauty,
   Now so late those charms I learn,
Now, at least, and ever, ever
   With thy love my heart will burn,
     For the Mother and the Child—
     Rose and Lily undefiled.

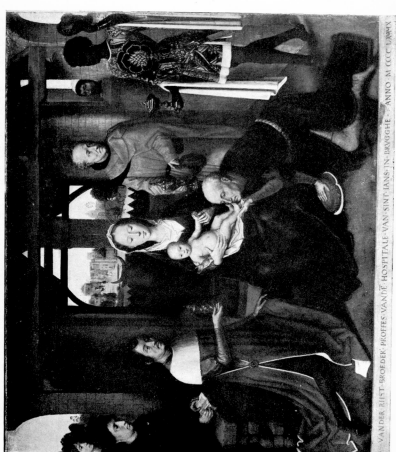

THE ADORATION OF THE MAGI

Memling

Plant and Fruit, and Fruit and Blossom—
  I am theirs, and they are mine ;
For no other prize I labour,
  For no other bliss I pine ;
    Love can every pain requite,
    Love alone is full delight.

ELIZABETH BARRETT BROWNING (1806-1861).

    Sleep, sleep, mine Holy One,
My flesh, my Lord—what name ?   I do not know
A name that seemeth not too high, or low,
    Too far from me, or heaven :
My Jesus, that is best—that word being given
By the majestic angel whose command
Was softly, as a man's beseeching, said,
When I and all the earth appeared to stand
    In the great overflow
Of light celestial from his wings and head.
    Sleep, sleep, my saving One.

And art thou come for saving, baby-browed
And speechless Being—art thou come for saving ?
The palm that grows beside our door is bowed
By treadings of the low wind from the south,
A restless shadow through the chamber waving :
Upon its bough a bird sings in the sun ;
But thou, with that close slumber on thy mouth,
Dost seem of wind and sun already weary.
Art thou come for saving, O my weary One ?

Perchance this sleep, that shutteth out the dreary
Earth-sounds and motions, opens on thy soul
    High dreams on fire with God ;
High songs that make the pathways where they roll
More bright than stars do theirs; and visions new
Of thine Eternal Nature's old abode.
    Suffer this Mother's kiss,
    Best thing that earthly is,
To glide the music and the glory through,
Nor narrow in thy dream the broad upliftings
    Of any seraph wing.
Thus, noiseless, thus.   Sleep, sleep, my dreaming One.

The slumber of his lips meseems to run
Through my lips to mine heart, to all its shiftings
Of sensual life, bringing contrariousness
In a great calm.   I feel I could lie down,
As Moses did, and die—and then live most.
I am 'ware of you, heavenly presences,
That stand with your peculiar light unlost,
Each forehead with a high thought for a crown,
Unsunned in the sunshine.   I am 'ware.   Ye throw
No shade against the wall.   How motionless
Ye round me with your living statuary,
While, through your whiteness, in and outwardly,
Continual thoughts of God appear to go,
Like light's soul in itself.   I bear, I bear
To look upon the dropt lids of your eyes,
Though their external shining testifies
To that beatitude, within which were
Enough to blast an eagle at his sun :

I fall not on my sad clay face before ye—
    I look on his.   I know
My spirit, which dilateth with the woe
    Of his mortality,
    May well contain your glory.
    Yea, drop your lids more low.
Ye are but fellow-worshippers with me.
    Sleep, sleep, my worshipped One.
We sate among the stalls at Bethlehem ;
The dumb kine from their fodder turning them,
    Softened their hornèd faces
    To almost human gazes
    Toward the Newly-born :
The simple shepherds from the star-lit brooks
    Brought visionary looks,
As yet, in their astonied hearing, rung
    The strange sweet angel tongue :

The Magi of the east, in sandals worn,
    Knelt reverent, sweeping round,
With long pale beards, their gifts upon the ground—
    The incense, myrrh and gold
These baby-hands were impotent to hold :
So, let all earthlies and celestials wait
    Upon thy royal state.
    Sleep, sleep, my kingly One.

I am not proud—meek angels, ye invest
New meeknesses to hear such utterance rest
On mortal lips—' I am not proud '—not proud :
Albeit, in my flesh God sent his Son ;
Albeit, over him my head is bowed

As others bow before him ; still, mine heart
Bows lower than their knees.

. . . . . .

I often wandered forth, more child than maiden,
Among the midnight hills of Galilee
    Whose summits looked heaven-laden,
Listening to silence, as it seemed to be
God's voice, so soft yet strong, so fain to press
Upon my heart, as heaven did on the height,
And waken up its shadows by a light,
And show its vileness by a holiness.
Then, I knelt down most silent like the night,
    Too self-renounced for fears,
Raising my small face to the boundless blue
Whose stars did mix and tremble in my tears :
God heard them falling after, with his dew.

. . . . . .

    Ah, King ; ah, Christ ; ah, Son :
    Sleep, sleep, my kingly One.

Art thou a King, then ?   Come, his universe,
    Come, crown me him a King,
Pluck rays from all such stars as never fling
    Their light where fell a curse,
And make a crowning for this kingly brow.
    Each empyreal star
    Sits in a sphere afar
    In shining ambuscade :
    The child-brow, crowned by none,
    Keeps its unchildlike shade.
    Sleep, sleep, my crownless One.

THE ADORATION OF THE MAGI

Rubens

Unchildlike shade.   No other babe doth wear
An aspect very sorrowful, as thou.
No small babe-smiles my watching heart has seen
To float like speech, the speechless lips between ;
No dovelike cooing in the golden air ;
No quick short joys of leaping babyhood ;
    Alas, our earthly good
In heaven thought evil, seems too good for thee :
    Yet, sleep, my weary One.

And then, the drear sharp tongue of prophecy,
With the dread sense of things which shall be done,
Doth smite me inly, like a sword : a sword ?
That, ' smites the Shepherd.'   Then, I think aloud
The words ' despised,' ' rejected '—every word
Recoiling into darkness, as I view
    The Darling on my knee.
Bright angels, move not—lest ye stir the cloud
Betwixt my soul and his futurity.
I must not die, with Mother's work to do,
    And could not live—and see.

    It is enough to bear
    This Image still and fair ;
    This Holier in sleep
    Than a saint at prayer ;
    This aspect of a Child
    Who never sinned, or smiled ;
    This Presence in an Infant's face ;
    This Sadness most like love,
    This Love than love more deep,

This Weakness like omnipotence—
It is so strong to move.
Awful in this watching place ;
Awful, what I see from hence—
A King, without regalia,
A God, without the thunder,
A Child, without the heart for play ;
Aye, a Creator, rent asunder
From his first glory, and cast away
On his own world—for me alone
To hold in hands created, crying, ' Son.'

That tear fell not on thee,
Beloved; yet, thou stirrest in thy slumber.
Thou, stirring not for glad sounds out of number
Which, through the vibratory palm-trees, run
From summer-wind and bird,
So quickly hast thou heard
A tear fall silently ?
Wak'st thou, O loving One ?

ALFRED NOYES (1880-).

SLUMBER-SONGS OF THE MADONNA.

PRELUDE.

Dante saw the great white Rose
Half unclose ;
Dante saw the golden bees
Gathering from its heart of gold
Sweets untold,
Love's most honeyed harmonies. . . .

THE ADORATION OF THE SHEPHERDS

Ribera

Something still remained, it seems,
In his dreams
Dante missed (as angels may
In their white and burning bliss)
Some small kiss
Mortals meet with every day.

Still on earth we pass and hear
Everywhere,
Hear, or see in silent eyes,
Just the song she still would sing
Thus, a-swing
O'er the cradle, where He lies :

I.

Sleep, little nestling, I love thee.
Sleep, little king.   I am bending above thee !
How should I know what to sing
Here, in my arms as I swing thee to sleep ?
Hushaby low,
Rockaby so,
Kings may have wonderful jewels to bring.
Mother has only a kiss for her king !
Why should my singing so make me to weep ?
Only I know that I love thee, I love thee,
Love thee, my little one,
Sleep.

II.

Is it a dream ?   Ah yet, it seems
Not the same as other dreams !

A ring of light was round thy head.
The great-eyed oxen nigh thy bed

H

Their innocent milk-white foreheads bowed.
Their sweet breath rose like an incense cloud
All round us in the lanthorn-light.
About the middle of the night
Through that dark open door-way, far
Above the hills, I saw a star. . . .

Then, with crimson gems a-flame,
Through the door the three kings came ;
And the black Ethiop unrolled
On this rough floor his cloth of gold,
And they poured forth before thee there,
Gold and frankincense and myrrh. . . .

III.

Ah, see, what a wonderful smile !   Does it mean
      That my little one knows of my love ?
Was it meant for an angel that passed unseen
      And smiled at us both from above ?
Does it mean that he knows of the birds and the flowers
That are waiting to sweeten his childhood's hours,
And the tales I shall tell, and the games he will play,
And the songs we shall sing, and the prayers we shall
      pray,
                  He and I, one day ?

IV.

      Many a day, O, many a day,
In the warm blue summer weather,
      Through the fields we two shall stray.
We shall laugh and love together.

THE PURIFICATION

Orcagna

I shall watch my little one growing,
I shall guide his feet,
  When the orange-trees are blowing
And the winds are heavy and sweet.
  When the orange-orchards whiten
  I shall see his great eyes brighten
To watch the long-legged camels going
  Up the twisted street,
When the orange trees are blowing
  And the winds are sweet.

We shall walk in pleasant vales
  Listening to the shepherd's song.
I shall tell him lovely tales
  All day long.
He shall laugh, while mother sings
Tales of fishermen and kings.

He shall see them come and go
  O'er the wistful sea,
Where rosy oleanders blow
  Round blue Lake Galilee,—
Kings with fishers' ragged coats,
And tawny nets across their boats,
Dipping through the starry glow
With crowns for him and me !
      Ah, no ;
Crowns for him, not me !

What does it mean ?   Indeed, it seems
A dream !   Yet not like other dreams !

V.

Child with the wonderful eyes
   (Wide open ! ah, not yet asleep !)
Wild miraculous eyes,
   Deep as the skies are deep,
Are there stars in your depths, are there tears,
Waiting down there, for the years
That shall wake you to love—and to weep ?
Ah, in that day, could I kiss you to sleep,
Then, little lips, little eyes,
Little lips that are lovely and wise,
Little lips that are dreadful and wise.

VI.

Ah, clenched little hands, so dear ;
Little brows so thoughtful and clear ;
Ah, smooth little side, so sweet,
And soft little unstained feet ;—
There is nothing—no, nothing—to fear.
I hear a shouting, far away,
You shall ride on a kingly palm-strewn way,
   One day, one triumphing day.

But, when you are crowned with a golden crown,
   And throned on a golden throne,
You 'll forget the manger of Bethlehem town
   And your mother that sits alone,
Wondering whether the mighty king
Remembers a song she used to sing,
     Long ago,—

' Rockaby so,
Kings may have wonderful jewels to bring.
Mother has only a kiss for her king ! ' . . .

Ah, see what a wonderful smile once more.
  He opens his great dark eyes.
Little child !   Little king !   Nay, hush, it is o'er,—
  My fear of those deep twin-skies.
    Little child,
  You are all too dreadful and wise.

But now you are mine, all mine ;
  And your feet can lie in my hand so small,
And your tiny hands in my heart can twine,
  And you cannot walk, so you never shall fall ;
Or be pierced by the thorns beside the door,
Or the nails that lie upon Joseph's floor.
Through sun and rain, through shadow and shine,
  You are mine, all mine.

V

THE CHILD JESUS

Thou . . . shalt call his name Jesus. He shall be great, and shall be called the Son of the Highest : and the Lord God shall give unto him the throne of his father David : and he shall reign over the house of Jacob for ever ; and of his kingdom there shall be no end.—*St. Luke* i. 31-33.

RICHARD CRASHAW (? 1613-1649).

That on her lap she cast her humble eye,
'Tis the sweet pride of her humility.
The fair star is well fixt, for where, O where
Could she have fixt it on a fairer sphere ?
'Tis Heaven, 'tis Heaven she sees, Heaven's God
   there lies ;
She can see Heaven, and ne'er lift up her eyes :
This new Guest to her eyes new laws hath given,
'Twas once, Look up, 'tis now, Look down, to
   Heaven.

ADAM SCOT (Twelfth Century).

O Child, Creator of all things, how humbly Thou liest in the manger, though Thou rulest in the heaven ! There the heaven of heavens cannot contain Thee, and here Thou art enclosed in a narrow crib. In the beginning of the world Thou didst clothe the earth with herbs and trees, springing up and bearing fruit ;

62

THE PRESENTATION IN THE TEMPLE

Mantegna

Thou didst adorn the firmament with sun and moon
and stars, and didst fill the air with birds, the waters
with fish, the earth with reptiles and with beasts.
And now at the end of the world Thou art wrapped
in swaddling clothes ! O majesty, O humility ; O
height, O depth ; O immense, eternal, O Ancient of
days ; yet, O little One, O Infant not yet a day old
upon the earth !

Rejoice and be glad, O Virgin. Thou embracest
Him whom the innumerable choirs of heavenly spirits
cannot comprehend as He lies in the bosom of His
Father. Now thou bowest down before Him as thy
Creator, then thou liftest Him up as an Infant ; now
thou salutest Him as thy Lord, then thou embracest
Him as thy Child ; now thou liest prostrate in soul
before Him as the Most High, and then thou smilest
on Him as a little one. O, rejoice and exult to-day
in Him to whom thou hast given birth. O sweet
Virgin, O gentle Virgin, assist us and protect us in the
terrible day of judgment, that as we have rejoiced in
His coming as our Redeemer, we may not tremble
when we see Him coming to be our judge.

SELWYN IMAGE (1849-).

> See, the lovely Babe asleep
>   On His Mother's milky breast :
>   Ah ! how tenderly caressed !
>
> Let us kneel, and vigil keep
>   At this quiet cradle-side :
>   Mother ! may we here abide ?

Verily, we 've naught to bring
  For an off'ring at His feet,
  Neither gold, nor incense sweet :

Nor a voice, wherewith to sing
  Lullaby to His repose,
  'Mid the winter storm and snows.

Only let us kneel, and pray
  Quietly, sweet Mother, here.
  Till the darkness disappear :

Till the Blessed One at day
  Waken ; till He hear us cry,
  Jesu, nobis subveni !

AUBREY THOMAS DE VERE (1814-1902).

I see him : on thy lap he lies
  'Mid that Judæan stable's gloom :
Oh, sweet, Oh, awful Sacrifice ;
  He smiles in sleep, yet knows the doom.

Thou gav'st him life : but, was not this
  That life which knows no parting breath ?
Unmeasured life ? unwaning bliss ?
  Dread Priestess, lo, thou gav'st him death.

Beneath the tree thy Mother stood ;
  Beneath the cross thou too shalt stand—
O tree of life, O bleeding rood,
  Thy shadow stretches far its hand.

That God who made the sun and moon,
  In swaddling bands lies dumb and bound—
Love's Captive, darker prison soon
  Awaits thee in the garden ground.

He wakens : Paradise looks forth
  Beyond the portals of the grave.
Life, life thou gavest—life to earth,
  Not him : thine Infant dies to save.

G. K. CHESTERTON (1874-).

  The Christ-Child lay on Mary's lap,
    His hair was like a light.
  (O weary, weary were the world,
    But here is all aright.)
  The Christ-Child lay on Mary's breast,
    His hair was like a star.
  (O stern and cunning are the Kings,
    But here the true hearts are.)
  The Christ-Child lay on Mary's heart,
    His hair was like a fire.
  (O weary, weary is the world,
    But here the world's desire.)
  The Christ-Child stood on Mary's knee,
    His hair was like a crown,
  And all the flowers looked up at Him,
    And all the stars looked down.

I

ALICE MEYNELL (1850-1922).

No sudden thing of glory and fear
Was the Lord's coming ; but the dear
Slow Nature's days followed each other
To form the Saviour from His Mother
—One of the Children of the year.
The earth, the rain, received the trust
—The sun and dews, to frame the Just.
He drew His daily life from these,
According to His own decrees
Who makes man from the fertile dust.
Sweet summer and the winter wild,
These brought Him forth, the Undefiled.
The happy Springs renewed again
His daily bread, the growing grain,
The food and raiment of the Child.

DORA GREENWELL (1821-1882).

O little blade of grass,
    A little sword thou art,
That, in thy haste to pass,
    Hast pierced thy Mother's heart.
O little blade of grass,
    A little tongue thou art
Of cleaving flame—alas,
    Thou hast cleft thy Mother's heart.
O little blade, upcurled
    Leaf, sword, or fiery dart,
To win thy Father's world
    Thou must break thy Mother's heart.

THE PRESENTATION IN THE TEMPLE

Rembrandt

CHRISTINA ROSSETTI (1830-1894).

   ' Lord Babe, if Thou art He
We sought for patiently,
Where is Thy court ? '
' Bow down and worship, righteous man :
This infant of a span.'

   .   .   .   .   .   .

' But wherefore dost Thou keep so mean a state
Low-lying desolate ? '
' Bow down and worship, righteous seer ;
The Lord our God is here
Approachable, who bids us all draw near.'

RICHARD CRASHAW (? 1613-1649).

Bright Babe ! Whose awful beauties make
The morn incur a sweet mistake,
For whom the officious Heavens devise
To disinherit the sun's rise,
Delicately to displace
The Day, and plant it fairer in Thy Face.

   .   .   .   .   .   .

Look up, sweet Babe, look up and see,
    For love of Thee,
Thus far from home
The East is come
To seek herself in Thy sweet eyes. . . .

O Little All ! in Thy embrace
The world lies warm, and likes his place.

JOHN DONNE (1573-1631).

With his kind Mother, who partakes thy woe,
Joseph, turn back : see, where your Child doth
    sit
Blowing, yea, blowing out those sparks of wit,
Which himself on those doctors did bestow.
The Word but lately could not speak ; and lo,
It suddenly speaks wonders.   Whence comes it,
That all which was, and all which would be, writ
A shallow-seeming Child should deeply know ?
His Godhead was not soul to his Manhood ;
Nor had time mellowed him to this ripeness ;
But, as for one which hath long tasks, 'tis good
With the sun to begin his business,
He, in his age's morning, thus began
By miracles exceeding power of man.

POPE LEO XIII. (1810-1903).

Now lamps our churches flood with light,
Now altars gleam with garlands bright,
Now censers, in sweet odours, raise
                Their pious praise.

'Twere sweet to sing, and well 'twere done,
The royal births of God's own Son,
Or David's ancient line, and see
                God's ancestry.

But sweeter Nazareth's lowly cot
To praise, and Jesus' humble lot ;
Or tell in words with sweetness rife
    His silent life.

Quick, Angel-led, from Nile's far shore
The wanderer is home once more :
The Boy, who evil days has passed,
    Is safe at last.

To youth grows Jesus, day by day
Passing His hidden life away,
And wills to learn, with Joseph's aid,
    His lowly trade.

' Toil,' said He, ' well may make Me sweat,
Who one day will with Blood be wet ;
Let this pain, too, cleanse, for it can,
    Poor, sinful man.'

The Mother sits her Son beside,
Near Joseph stays his Virgin-Bride,
Their happy handmaid, making less
    Their weariness.

VI

JOSEPH AND MARY

And Mary said, . . . he hath regarded the low estate of his
handmaiden.—*St. Luke* i. 48.

St. Epiphanius (320-400).

From the root of Jesse sprung king David, and from
the family of king David the holy Virgin : holy, I
say, and daughter of holy men.   Her parents were
Joachim and Anne, who pleased God in their life, and
bore like fruit, even the holy Virgin Mary, at once the
temple and Mother of God.   These three, moreover,
Joachim, Anne, and Mary, offered to the Trinity a
sacrifice of praise.   For Joachim is interpreted the
preparation of the Lord, since from him it was that the
temple of the Lord was prepared, namely, the Virgin.
Anne is interpreted grace, because Joachim and Anne
received grace, after having prayed, to bear such fruit,
by obtaining the holy Virgin.   For whilst Joachim
prayed on the mountain, Anne prayed in her garden.
Anne then conceived, and gave birth to a heaven and
throne of cherubim, the holy child Mary.   For she
will be found to be a heaven, a temple, and a throne,
since we are wont to interpret Mary, Lady and also
hope.   For she gave birth to the Lord, who is the
Hope of the whole world, that is, Christ.

JOACHIM AND ANNA AT THE GOLDEN GATE

Maître de Moulins

JAMES THE MONK (Eleventh Century).

Such were the gains and the deeds of the righteous (Joachim and Anne) ; such the bright characters of their virtues, who inflashed the noble beauty of soul brighter than those who had appeared before them. For need was that that incomparable gift among those begotten should proceed from a supereminent election ; need was that that hyper-holy wealth should weigh down from abundant virtues ; need was that such a fruit should be gathered from such pains, that from a noble root should the noblest germ be put forth ; that from good loins should that best foetus be yielded, the ever-green ornament of the race, the most beauteous germ of the nature, the upstretching stem of the mystery, from which the Flower of immortality ascending diffused the eternal sweetness, whose Fruit is made life and incorruption and abidingness to all who partake of it. How blessed the election, most blessed their distinction in virtues, through which the election came to them ; for this it was vouchsafed to them to produce the Queen of all, as the fruit of piety and strength. For need was that from royal plantations shouldest thou be yielded, the royal scion : need was that from abundant virtues shouldest thou, the abundant wealth of good things, be poured out ; need was that thou shouldest be the daughter of such parents, and that they should be the parents of such a daughter. For as thou wast fore-elected before all creation to be mother of God, so was it vouchsafed to them to be preferred to all parents. How more glorious is the magnificence of Providence ! how more desirable than all objects of desire the excellent things which came through thee !

ARTHUR M. MORGAN (1855).

There are who in the night lie down to slumber,
And, waking, joy to know their grief a dream ;
There are who wake and work beneath the gleam,
Yet, sleep—such phantasies their noonday cumber.
There is who, coming in the midnight sombre,
Tells men of heaven beneath the clouds begun,
And bids them sorrows with their dreams to number,
Which fade, and fading, bring to them the sun.
Sleep, sleep, O Joseph ; thou didst dream while
    waking,
Thou in thy slumber things of day shalt hear ;
The star of morning says the sun is breaking,
The angel speaks the King of angels near.
O Foster-Father, guard thy household well—
The Ever-Maiden, the Immanuel.

ST. ALPHONSUS MARIA DE LIGUORI (1696-1787).

Raise your voices, vales and mountains,
Flowery meadows, streams and fountains,
    Praise, oh, praise the loveliest Maiden
        Ever the Creator made.
Murmuring brooks, your tribute bringing,
Little birds with joyful singing,
    Come with mirthful praises laden—
        To your Queen be homage paid.

THE FLIGHT INTO EGYPT

Giotto

Say, sweet Virgin, we implore thee,
Say, what beauty God sheds o'er thee :
   Praise and thanks to him be given,
     Who in love created thee.
Like a sun with splendour glowing,
Gleams thy heart with love o'erflowing ;
   Like the moon in starry heaven,
     Shines thy peerless purity.

Like the rose and lily blooming,
Sweetly heaven and earth perfuming,
   Stainless, spotless, thou appearest—
     Queenly beauty graces thee.
But, to God, in whom thou livest,
Sweeter joy and praise thou givest,
   When to him in beauty nearest,
     Yet, so humble thou canst be.

MARY ELIZABETH COLERIDGE (1861-1907).

Mother of God ! no lady thou :
Common woman of common earth !
Our Lady ladies call thee now,
But Christ was never of gentle birth ;
A common man of the common earth.

For God's ways are not as our ways,
The noblest lady of the land
Would have given up half her days,
Would have cut off her right hand,
To bear the Child that was God of the land.

K

Never a lady did He choose,
Only a maid of low degree,
So humble she might not refuse
The carpenter of Galilee.
A daughter of the people, she.

Out she sang the song of her heart.
Never a lady had so sung.
She knew no letters, had no art ;
To all mankind, in woman's tongue,
Hath Israelitish Mary sung.

And still for men to come she sings,
Nor shall her singing pass away.
He hath filled the hungry with good things—
Oh, listen, lords and ladies gay !—
And the rich He hath sent empty away.

WILLIAM WORDSWORTH (1770-1850).

Mother, whose virgin bosom was uncrost
With the least shade of thought to sin allied ;
Woman, above all women glorified,
Our tainted nature's solitary boast ;
Purer than foam on central ocean tost ;
Brighter than eastern skies at daybreak strewn
With fancied roses, than the unblemished moon
Before her wane begins on heaven's blue coast,
The image falls to earth.

THE FLIGHT INTO EGYPT

Yet some, I ween,
Not unforgiven the suppliant knee might bend,
As to a visible power, in which did blend
All that was mixed and reconciled in thee
Of mother's love with maiden purity,
Of high with low, celestial with terrene.

DANTE (1265-1321).

O Virgin Mother, daughter of thy Son,
Created beings all in lowliness
Surpassing, as in height above them all :
Term by th' eternal Council pre-ordain'd
Ennobler of thy nature, so advanced
In thee, that its great Maker did not scorn
Himself in His own work enclosed to dwell.
For in thy womb rekindling shone the love
Reveal'd, whose genial influence makes now
This flow'r to germ in Eternal peace :
Hence thou to us of charity and love
Art as the noonday touch, and art beneath
To mortal men of hope a living spring.
So mighty art thou, lady, and so great,
That he who grace desireth, and comes not
To thee for aidance, fain would have desire
Fly without wings ; nor only him who asks
Thy bounty, succours, but both freely oft
Forerun the asking ; whatsoe'er may be
Of excellence in creatures—pity mild,
Relenting mercy, large munificence
Are all combined in thee.

ROBERT BRIDGES, POET LAUREATE (1844-).

Madonna ! azure-mantled and aureoled
That standing barefoot upon the moon
    Or throned as a Queen of the earth
    Tranquilly smilest to hold
    The Child-god in thine arms,
Whence thy glory ?   Art not she
The country maiden of Galilee
Simple in dowerless poverty
Who from humble cradle to grave
    Hadst no thought of this wonder ?

    When to man dull of heart
    Dawn'd at length graciously
    Thy might of Motherhood
The starry Truth beam'd on his home ;
Then with insight exalted he gave thee
The trappings—Lady—wherewith his art
Delighteth to picture his spirit to sense
    And that grace is immortal.

    Fount of creative Love
    Mother of the Word eternal
    Atoning man with God :
Who set thee apart as a garden enclosed
From Nature's all-producing wilds
To rear the richest fruit o' the Life
Ever continuing out from Him
    Urgent since the beginning.

Behold !   Man setteth thine image in the
  height of Heaven
And hallowing his untemper'd love
    Crowneth and throneth thee ador'd
    (Tranquilly joyous to hold
    The man-child in thine arms)
God-like apart from conflict to save thee
To guard thy weak caressive beauty
With incontaminate jewels of soul
Courage, patience, and self-devotion :
    All this glory he gave thee.

    Secret and slow is Nature
    Imperceptibly moving
    With surely determinate aim :
To woman it fell to be early in prime
Ready to labour, mould, and cherish
The delicate head of all Production
The wistful late-maturing boy [1]
    Who made Knowing of Being.

    Therefore art thou ador'd
    Mother of God in man
    Naturing nurse of power :
They who adore not thee shall perish
But thou shalt keep thy path of joy
Envied of Angels because the All-father
Call'd thee to mother his nascent Word
    And complete the creation.

      [1] Man-child not Christ.

GERARD MANLEY HOPKINS (1844-1889).
Mary Mother of Divine Grace, compared to the
air we breathe.

Wild air, world-mothering air,
Nestling me everywhere,
That each eyelash or hair
Girdles ; goes home betwixt
The fleeciest, frailest-flixed
Snow-flake ; that 's fairly mixed
With riddles, and is rife
In every least thing's life ;
This needful, never spent
And nursing element ;
My more than meat and drink,
My meal at every wink ;
This air which by life's law
My lung must draw and draw
Now, but to breathe its praise,—
Minds me in many ways
Of her who not only
Gave God's infinity,
Dwindled to infancy,
Welcome in womb and breast,
Birth, milk, and all the rest,
But mothers each new grace
That does not reach our race,
Mary Immaculate,
Merely a woman, yet
Whose presence, power is
Great as no goddess's

THE FLIGHT INTO EGYPT

Murillo

Was deemèd, dreamèd ; who
This one work has to do—
Let all God's glory through,
God's glory, which would go
Thro' her and from her flow
Off, and no way but so.
    I say that we are wound
With mercy round and round
As if with air : the same
Is Mary, more by name,
She, wild web, wondrous robe,
Mantles the guilty globe.
Since God has let dispense
Her prayers His providence.
Nay, more than almoner,
The sweet alms' self is her
And men are meant to share
Her life as life does air.
    If I have understood,
She holds high motherhood
Towards all our ghostly good,
And plays in grace her part
About man's beating heart,
Laying like air's fine flood
The death-dance in his blood ;
Yet no part but what will
Be Christ our Saviour still.
Of her flesh He took flesh :
He does take, fresh and fresh,
Though much the mystery how,
Not flesh but spirit now,

And wakes, O marvellous !
New Nazareths in us,
Where she shall yet conceive
Him, morning, noon, and eve ;
New Bethlems, and He born
There, evening, noon and morn.
Bethlem or Nazareth,
Men here may draw like breath
More Christ, and baffle death ;
Who, born so, comes to be
New self, and nobler me
In each one, and each one
More makes, when all is done,
Both God's and Mary's son.
    Again look overhead
How air is azurèd.
O how !   Nay, do but stand
Where you can lift your hand
Skywards : rich, rich it laps
Round the four finger gaps.
Yet such a sapphire-shot
Charged, steepèd sky will not
Stain light.   Yea, mark you this :
It does no prejudice.
The glass-blue days are those
When every colour glows,
Each shape and shadow shows.
Blue be it : this blue heaven
The seven or seven times seven
Hued sunbeam will transmit
Perfect, nor alter it.

THE REST ON THE FLIGHT INTO EGYPT

Albert Dürer

Or if there does some soft
On things aloof, aloft,
Bloom breathe, that one breath more
Earth is the fairer for.
Whereas did air not make
This bath of blue and slake
This fire, the sun would shake
A blear and blinding ball
With blackness bound, and all
The thick stars round him roll,
Flashing like flecks of coal,
Quartz-fret, or sparks of salt
In grimy vasty vault.
   So God was God of old ;
A mother came to mould
Those limbs like ours which are,
What must make our daystar
Much dearer to mankind :
Whose glory bare would blind
Or less would win man's mind.
Through her we may see Him
Made sweeter, not made dim,
And her hand leaves His light
Sifted to suit our sight.
   Be thou, then, O thou dear
Mother, my atmosphere ;
My happier world wherein
To wend and meet no sin ;
Above me, round me lie
Fronting my froward eye
With sweet and scarless sky ;

L

Stir in my ears, speak there
Of God's love, O live air,
Of patience, penance, prayer ;
World-mothering air, air wild,
Wound with thee, in thee isled,
Fold home, fast fold thy child.

JOANNES WATTON (? 1480).

Mary mother, well thou be !
Mary mother, think on me ;
Maiden and mother was never none
Together, Lady, save thee alone.
Sweet Lady, maiden clean,
Shield me from ill, shame and teen ;
Out of sin, Lady, shield thou me,
And out of debt for charity.
Lady, for thy joyes five,
Get me grace in this live
To know and keep over all thing,
Christian faith and God's bidding.
And truly win all that I need
To me and mine clothe and feed.
Help me, Lady, and all mine ;
Shield me, Lady, from hell pine ;
Shield me, Lady, from villainy,
And from all wicked company.

POPE LEO XIII. (1810-1903).

O Happy and august abode
    That once made Nazareth so blest,

The infant Church its nurture owed
  To thy most hospitable breast.

The sun that, with its golden light,
  Wide o'er the earth so loves to roam,
Has never seen so sweet a sight
  As this delightful, holy home.

Here, from the palace of the sky,
  Flock messengers on frequent wing ;
They come, and come again, thereby
  The shrine of virtue honouring.

With ready hand and right goodwill,
  Doth Jesus Joseph's wishes do :
How Mary doth, with rapturous thrill,
  A mother's household tasks pursue.

Joseph is near his spouse ; and he
  In all her love and care partakes :
The Source of virtue graciously
  'Twixt them a thousand love-ties makes.

They, mutually loving, turn
  Their loves to Jesus, both in one ;
And, making both their bosoms burn,
  His love rewards their unison.

May charity, that ne'er will cease,
  Between us, too, firm bonds create,
And, fostering thus domestic peace,
  Life, life so hard, alleviate.

Jesus, who an obedient Son
　　Unto Thy parents will to be,
With Father and with Spirit one,
　　Be glory evermore to Thee.

TE, JOSEPH, CELEBRENT (Seventeenth Century).

Joseph, to tell thy praise, let all the Angels sing ;
Let quiring Christendom their songs of thee repeat ;
The glorious Virgin's spouse who merited to be
　　　　In virgin wedlock sweet.

When, as her gracious Fruit was growing day by day,
Thy soul in sore amaze now this, now that believed,
An Angel, whispering, said that by the Holy Ghost
　　　　Her Babe had been conceived.

Thy arms thy new-born Lord most lovingly enfold ;
Thou fleest as He flees to Egypt's alien shore ;
Thou in Jerusalem, when He is lost, dost find,
　　　　And grief turns joy once more.

We, only after death, the heavenly palm obtain,
But thou in life wert made the peer of Saints above :
Thy happier lot it was thy God on earth to see
　　　　And love with wondering love.

Be clement to our prayer, O Trinity supreme !
Grant us, for Joseph's sake, the starry heights to
　　scale ;
That of Thy name at last, in songs of gratitude,
　　　　Our praise may never fail.

Iste, Quem Laeti (Seventeenth Century).

Joseph, whom gladly we, the faithful, honour,
Hymning the praise of so sublime a triumph,
This very day once merited to enter
   Bliss everlasting.

Happy, thrice happy, blessèd, oh ! thrice blessèd
He who, when mortal life was near its ending,
Jesus and Mary had, to watch beside him,
   Smiling serenely.

Hell overcoming thus, from flesh unfettered,
Calm and in slumber, to his home eternal
Lo ! he has passed, about his brows entwining
   Glorious garlands.

Then, let us beg him from his throne in Heaven,
Hither to come and, for our faults and failings
Pardon obtaining, grant us peace supernal,
   Gifted so greatly.

Glory and praise be Thine, O thou, the Triune,
O'er us who reignest as our God, and crownest
Servants found faithful with Thy crowns all golden,
   Splendid for ever.

H. N. Oxenham (1829-1888).

Who kneel to Mary, kneel to Mary's Son,
And therefore to the Mother-Maid we cry
Because her Son is God ; no rite profane,
No goddess-worshipping idolatry

Is ours ; to Him due honour we accord
Unlimited, unquestioning, entire,
The perfect service of obedient love ;
To her such limited and mediate power
As may befit a creature glorified,
Brightest and purest of the white-robed band
Who stand for aye before the throne of God,
One who perchance may pour, and not in vain,
An intercession for the little flock
Purchased by Jesu's all-redeeming blood.

ANONYMOUS.

Mary the Dawn, Christ the perfect Day :
Mary the Gate, Christ the heavenly Way.

Mary the Root, Christ the mystic Vine :
Mary the Grape, Christ the sacred Wine.

Mary the Corn-sheaf, Christ the living Bread :
Mary the Rose-tree, Christ the Rose blood-red.

Mary the Fount, Christ the cleansing Flood :
Mary the Chalice, Christ the saving Blood.

Mary the Temple, Christ the temple's Lord :
Mary the Shrine, Christ its God adored.

Mary the Beacon, Christ the Heaven's Rest :
Mary the Mirror, Christ the Vision blest.

THE VIRGIN AND CHILD
French, c. 1300

AUBREY THOMAS DE VERE (1814-1902).

> Who doubts that thou art finite ?   Who
>   Is ignorant that from Godhead's height
> To what is loftiest here below
>   The interval is infinite ?
>
> O Mary ! with that smile thrice-blest
>   Upon their petulance look down ;
> Their dull negation, blind protest ;
>   Thy smile will melt away their frown.
>
> Show them thy Son !   That hour their heart
>   Will beat and burn with love like thine ;
> Grow large ; and learn from thee that art
>   Which communes best with things divine.

J. M. NEALE (1818-1866).

> Royal day that chasest gloom,
>   Day by gladness speeded :
> Thou beheld'st from Mary's womb
>   How the King proceeded :
> . Very God, Who made the sky
> Set the sun and stars on high,
>   Heaven and earth sustaining :
> Very Man Who freely bare
> Toil and sorrow, woe and care,
>   Man's salvation gaining.

As the sunbeam through the glass
  Passeth, but not staineth,
Thus the Virgin, as she was,
  Virgin still remaineth ;
Blessed Mother in whose womb
Lay the Light that exiles gloom,
  God to earth descending ;
Blessèd Maid whose spotless breast
Gives the King of Glory rest,
  Nurture, warmth, and tending.

Christ, Who mad'st us out of dust,
  Breath and spirit giving ;
Christ, from Whose dear steps we must
  Pattern take of living ;
Christ, Who camest once to save
From the curse and from the grave,
  Healing, lightening, cheering :
Christ, Who now wast made as we,
Grant that we may be like Thee
  In thy next appearing !

CHRISTINA ROSSETTI (1830-1894).

Herself a rose, who bore the Rose,
  She bore the Rose and felt its thorn,
  All Loveliness new-born
Took on her bosom its repose,
  And slept and woke there night and morn.

THE VIRGIN AND CHILD

Donatello

Lily herself, she bore the one
  Fair Lily ; sweeter, whiter, far
  Than she or others are :
The Sun of Righteousness her Son,
  She was His morning star.

She gracious, He essential Grace,
  He was the Fountain, she the rill :
  Her goodness to fulfil
And gladness, with proportioned pace
  He led her steps thro' good and ill.

Christ's mirror she of grace and love,
  Of beauty and of life and death :
  By hope and love and faith
Transfigured to His Likeness ' Dove
  Spouse, Sister, Mother,' Jesus saith.

J. B. BOSSUET (1627-1704).

Many portraits have been painted of Mary, by
many artists, each painting her according to his own
idea. There can, however, be only one true likeness
of her : namely, a copy of her character as shown forth
in the Gospels, the account of which forms a portrait
drawn, if we may venture to say so, by the Holy Spirit
Himself. And what is the character thus set before
us in Scripture ? It is neither Mary's high intercourse with God, nor her great and special graces, nor
her power. All these are kept in the background.
What is brought before us is simply her ordinary

M

every-day virtues, that she may be a model for daily, familiar use. Now, the essence of Mary's character, as thus displayed, is her modesty and self-restraint. She never thinks of showing herself, though she was doubtless beautiful ; nor of decking herself, though young ; nor of exalting herself, though noble ; nor of enriching herself, though poor.

Thoughtful and prudent, modest, self-restrained, humble, and unselfish—is this Virgin, of whom I repeat that we can never be her clients if we are not also her followers.

BISHOP ULLATHORNE (1806-1889).

Mary is the highest example of human perfection and of created happiness. And this great fact strikes down a thousand theories. In every earthly sense of the word she is weak, as she is lowly, poor and humble ; and yet she is perfect as no one else ever was perfect. And her perfection is the work of a sublime grace, which puts her nature in order and sets her higher powers free in God. The Immaculate Conception is the mystery of God's strength in weakness, of His height in humility, of His glory in purity. And when we contemplate that glorious creature, in whom from the first instant of her creation the image of God was so beautiful, in whom grace found no resistance, whose aspirations grew ever more divine ; when we con-template that living shrine of the Holy Spirit's fire ; when we look up to that animated temple of the Divinity, and behold her immaculate brightness, as

THE VIRGIN AND CHILD

Florentine, c. 1460

clothed with the sun and crowned with the stars, and seated next her Son above Cherub and Seraph ; and when we hear her truthful lips proclaim : ' The Lord hath looked down upon the humility of His hand-maid. . . . He hath lifted up the lowly ' ; our pride sinks down rebuked, our false ambition stands re-proved, our sensuous strength betrays the weakness of its origin, and our confidence in the perfection of our nature is discovered to be that broken reed of which we had so often heard in vain. The condition of perfection is shown to be chaste humility, and the source of perfection the grace of Christ. And that grace must come to us as Christ prescribes, and not as we choose.

ALICE MEYNELL (1850-1922).

Of all reflective glory the glory of the Mother of Christ is the supreme example—so perfect an example that it might rather be called the solitary pattern. Have some enthusiasts seemed—whether they were poets writing sonnets in honour of the moon or Christians singing hymns in honour of Mary—to give their more sensible tenderness to the secondary splendour, have they seemed to forget that the moon-light is the sunlight simply returned, and Mary a moon to the sun of Christ, they have only seemed. The consciousness of God as the giver, the giver of all, lay immovably deep in the heart of the peasant saying ten ' Aves ' to one ' Pater Noster.' Nay, the case of Mary is singular in this entire humility and humilia-

tion. For we may all irrationally and nearly uncon-
sciously attribute some glory of genius to the poet,
for instance, as though it were his own by origin ; but
in the case of the Mother of Christ there is no such
vague illusion. The little idolatries that are offered
to the poet or the soldier are withheld from her who
is pre-eminent only for sanctity bestowed, and dis-
tinguished only by her office assigned, the preparation
therefor, and the reward thereafter. And this similitude of Mary and the moon is so perfect, that it is a
wonder the simple should need, or the churches erect,
images of the Virgin of Nazareth, the Virgin of the
Annunciation, the Mother of the Seven Sorrows, or
Our Lady of Peace, or the Mother of Christ by His
Cross, or Mary under any invocation whatever, when,
month by month, newly lighted every month, the
moon presents her absolute similitude, her image with
the superscription of her Lord. The natural love of
all ages for a Mother is obviously older than the
Christian love of nineteen centuries for a perpetual
Virgin. Therefore Mary, her Virginity receiving all
its mystery and all its singular glory from the fact of
her Maternity, is closest to the heart of sorrowful
mankind by the title of Mother.

CARDINAL NEWMAN (1801-1890).

Mary is exalted for the sake of Jesus. It was fitting
that she, as being a creature, though the first of
creatures, should have an office of ministration. She,
as others, came into the world to do a work, she had a

mission to fulfil ; her grace and her glory are not for her own sake, but for her Maker's ; and to her is committed the custody of the Incarnation ; this is her appointed office—' A Virgin shall conceive, and bear a Son, and they shall call His Name Emmanuel.' As she was once on earth, and was personally the guardian of her Divine Child, as she carried Him in her womb, folded Him in her embrace, and suckled Him at her breast, so now, and to the latest hour of the Church, do her glories and the devotion paid her proclaim and define the right faith concerning Him as God and man. Every church which is dedicated to her, every altar which is raised under her invocation, every image which represents her, every litany in her praise, every Hail Mary for her continual memory, does but remind us that there was One who, though He was all-blessed from all eternity, yet for the sake of sinners ' did not shrink from the Virgin's womb.'

JEAN BAPTISTE DE SANTEUIL (1630-1697).

 1. *Stupete, gentes, fit Deus hostia.*

Ye wondering nations, see
 The Ruler of the skies,
Oh, most amazing mystery,
 His people's Sacrifice.

The Law's own Lord obeys
 The ordinance he gave ;
A price is paid for him who pays
 A price the world to save.

And she, the spotless Maid,
   Performs the stern command ;
The Shrine of God—and yet, afraid
   Within his courts to stand.

An agèd saint appears
   His humble gift to bring,
And give his few remaining years
   To join the offering.

O Maid, what anguish fierce
   Remaineth yet for thee,
Whose tender heart the sword shall pierce,
   Beside the dreadful tree—

Where thou, whose Infant cries
   Foretell thy future woe,
Shalt die, the perfect Sacrifice,
   Redeeming all below.

Then let us love thee well,
   And praise thee evermore ;
Let all the Father's praises tell ;
   The Holy Ghost adore.

2. *Templi sacratas pande, Sion, fores.*

O Sion, ope thy temple-gates ;
See, Christ, the Priest and Victim, waits—
   Let Lifeless shadows flee :
No more to heaven shall vainly rise
The ancient rites—a sacrifice
   All pure and perfect, see.

THE VIRGIN AND CHILD
School of Verrocchio

Behold, the Maiden knowing well
The hidden Godhead that doth dwell
 In him her infant Son :
And with her Infant, see her bring
The doves, the humble offering
 For Christ, the Holy One.

Here, all who for his coming sighed
Behold him, and are satisfied—
 Their faith the prize hath won :
While Mary in her breast conceals
The holy joys her Lord reveals
 And ponders them alone.

ASCRIBED TO ARCHBISHOP RABANUS MAURUS (Ninth
 Century).

All prophets hail thee, from of old announcing,
By the inbreathèd spirit of the Father,
God's Mother, bringing prophecies to fullness,
 Mary the maiden.

Thou the true Virgin Mother of the Highest,
Bearing incarnate God in awed obedience,
Meekly acceptest for a sinless offspring
 Purification.

In the high temple Simeon receives thee,
Takes in his agèd arms with holy rapture
That promised Saviour, vision of redemption,
 Christ long awaited.

Now the fair realm of Paradise attaining,
And to thy Son's throne, Mother of the Eternal,
Raisèd all glorious, yet in earth's devotion
    Join with us always.

Glory and worship to the Lord of all things
Pay we unresting, who alone adorèd,
Father and Son and Spirit, in the highest
    Reigneth eternal.   Amen.

JOHN FITZPATRICK (1859-).

    My Lady is a fragrant rose,
    And near to God my Lady grows ;
    And all my thoughts are murmuring bees
    That haste in silent ecstasies
    Upon her beauty to repose
    Sweeter than any flower that blows,
    Since all the scents her lips disclose
    Are prayers upon the heavenly breeze,
        My Lady is.

    Her summer never comes and goes ;
    And, for the sweetness she bestows,
    My heart's the hive where by degrees
    I hoard my golden memories ;
    For Mary, as my angel knows,
        My Lady is.

ADELAIDE A. PROCTER (1825-1864).

    Around thy starry crown are wreathed
    So many names divine :

THE MADONNA OF THE MAGNIFICAT

Botticelli

Which is the dearest to my heart,
    And the most worthy thine ?

.   .   .   .   .

Mary : the dearest name of all,
    The holiest and the best ;
The first low word that Jesus lisped
    Laid on His mother's breast.

Mary, the name that Gabriel spoke,
    The name that conquers hell ;
Mary, the name that through high heaven
    The angels love so well.

.   .   .   .   .

Mary—our comfort and our hope.
    Oh, may that word be given
To be the last we sigh on earth—
    The first we breathe in heaven.

St. Bernard (1091-1153).

There can be no doubt that whatever we utter in
praise of the Mother belongs to her Son, and also
that when we praise the Son we are proclaiming the
glory of His Mother.

N

VII

HAIL, FULL OF GRACE

Hail, thou that art highly favoured, the Lord is with thee: blessed art thou among women.—St. Luke i. 28.

JOHN GEOMETRA (Ninth Century).

Hail, O form, framed from above, from the starry
  heaven,
  Drawing nothing of daily evil ;
Hail, O form, tempered, hitherto undefiled in each
  way ;
  Of beauty aerial, of beauty from this earth ;
Hail, O form, like a chariot of fire, hiding another
  Sun,
  The everliving Lord of the Sun ;
Hail, grace, Mother of Wisdom, of Light, of Word,
  of Might,
  Mother of the Father, daughter of thy Son ;
Hail, delight of God, new chariot of the Allwise,
  Where the sun ran its course to our setting ;
Hail, thou pregnant of the welcomed Word, self-
  produced,
  Of the self-engendering light, the primæval
  Nature ;

MADONNA AND CHILD

Michelangelo

Hail, thou who gavest bodily substance to God, and
    again
Hail thou, who cleansedst from grievous grossness
    unto God.

ST. EPHREM (Fourth Century).

Deign that I too, thy humble servant, praise thee, O
sacred Virgin, and with sweet devotion say : Hail,
thou glorious and elect vessel of God.   Hail, amongst
women Virgin most blessèd.   Hail, most brightly
shining star from whom Christ came forth.   Hail,
thou who wondrously gavest birth to the Monarch of
the universe.   Hail, Queen and Mistress, of all the
most sublime.   Hail, thou canticle of cherubim and
seraphim, and hymnody of angels.   Hail, peace, joy,
consolation, and salvation of the world.   Hail, praise
of the patriarchs, and glory of the prophets.   Hail,
beauty of martyrs, and crown of saints.   Hail, glory
and praise of the pious who live in solitude. . . .
Hail, thou charm of all the earth-born.   Hail, paradise
of pleasure and immortality.

Hail, most tranquil haven, and most ardently longed-
for rescuer of the tempest-tossed from billows and
storms. . . .   Hail, sweet solace and protection of the
converted.   Hail, most efficacious peace-maker of the
whole world.   Hail, our Lady who by thy prayers
obtainest for thy faithful ones a covenant, peace, and
a sceptre wherewith to rule all. . . . Hail, thou by
whom are unlocked the gates of the celestial paradise.
Hail, our consoler who hast assuaged the griefs and

calmed the troubles of the afflicted.   Hail, most safe
port of voyagers here on earth.   Hail, our universal
protection and glory.   Hail, thou who didst rear
Christ the giver of Life ; Christ, I say, the most
merciful Creator of all things, our most sweet Lord
Jesus, the rearer and nourisher of the whole world,
the most gracious lover of mankind, and Almighty
Father of all.

PERCY BYSSHE SHELLEY (1792-1822).

    Seraph of Heaven, too gentle to be human,
    Veiling beneath that radiant form of Woman
    All that is insupportable in Thee
    Of light and love and immortality :
    Sweet Benediction in the eternal curse ;
    Veiled Glory of this lampless universe ;
    Thou Moon beyond the clouds ; thou living Form
    Among the dead ; thou Star above the storm ;
    Thou Wonder, and thou Beauty, and thou Terror ;
    Thou Harmony of nature's art ; thou Mirror
    In whom, as in the splendour of the sun,
    All shapes look glorious which thou gazest on ;
    Aye, even the dim worlds which obscure thee now
    Flash, lightning-like, with unaccustomed glow—
    I pray thee that thou blot from this sad song
    All of its much mortality and wrong,
    With those clear drops which start like sacred dew
    From the twin lights thy sweet soul darkens through,
    Weeping, till sorrow becomes ecstasy :
    Then smile on it, so that it may not die.

HENRY VAUGHAN (1622-1695).

Bright Queen of Heaven, God's Virgin Spouse,
  The glad world's blessèd Maid !
Whose beauty tied life to thy house,
  And brought us saving aid.

Thou art the true Love's-knot ; by thee
  God is made our ally ;
And man's inferior essence He
  With His did dignify.

For coalescent by that band
  We are His body grown,
Nourished with favours from His hand
  Whom for our Head we own.

And such a knot, what arm dares loose,
  What life, what death can sever ?
Which us in Him, and Him in us,
  United keeps for ever.

HENRY CONSTABLE (1562-1615).

In that, O Queen of Queens ! thy birth was free
From guilt, which others do of grace bereave,
When, in their mother's womb, they life receive
God, as His sole-borne Daughter, lovèd thee.
To match thee, like thy birth's nobility,
He thee His Spirit for thy Spouse did leave,
Of whom thou didst His only Son conceive,
And so wast linked to all the Trinity.

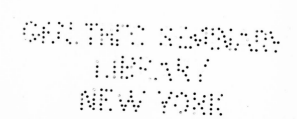

Sovereign of Queens ! if vain ambition move
My heart to seek an earthly prince's grace,
Show me thy Son in His imperial place,
Whose servants reign our kings and queens above :
And if alluring passions I do prove
By pleasing sighs, show me thy lovely face,
Whose beams the angels' beauty do deface,
And even inflame the seraphims with love.

So by ambition I shall humble be
When, in the presence of the highest King,
I serve all His, that He may honour me.
And love my heart to chaste desires shall bring,
When fairest Queen looks on me from her throne
And, jealous, bids me love but her alone.

  .   .   .   .   .   .

Sweet Queen ! although thy beauty raise up me
From sight of baser beauties here below,
Yet let me not rest there, but higher go
To Him, who took His shape from God and thee.
And if thy form in Him more fair I see,
What pleasure from His Deity shall flow,
By whose fair beams His beauty shineth so,
When I shall it behold eternally.

CARDINAL NEWMAN (1801-1890).

'Non horruisti Virginis uterum,' as the Church
sings, ' Thou didst not disdain the Virgin's womb.'
He took the substance of His human flesh from her,
and clothed in it He lay within her ; and He bore
it about with Him after birth, as a sort of badge

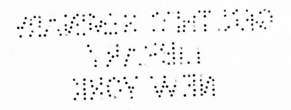

MADONNA AND CHILD

J. Bellini

and witness that He, though God, was hers.   He was nursed and tended by her ; He was suckled by her ; He lay in her arms.   As time went on, He ministered to her, and obeyed her.   He lived with her for thirty years, in one house, with an uninterrupted intercourse, and with only the saintly Joseph to share it with Him. She was the witness of His growth, of His joys, of His sorrows, of His prayers ; she was blest with His smile, with the touch of His hand, with the whisper of His affection, with the expression of His thoughts and His feelings, for that length of time.   Now what ought she to be, what is it becoming that she should be, who was so favoured ?   I answer, as the king was answered : Nothing is too high for her to whom God owes His human life ;   no exuberance of grace, no excess of glory, but is becoming, but is to be expected there, where God has lodged Himself, whence God has issued. Let her ' be clad in the king's apparel,' that is, let the fulness of the Godhead so flow into her that she may be a figure of the incommunicable sanctity, and beauty, and glory, of God Himself :   that she may be the Mirror of Justice, the Mystical Rose, the Tower of Ivory, the House of Gold, the Morning Star.   Let her ' receive the king's diadem upon her head,' as the Queen of heaven, the Mother of all living, the Health of the weak, the Refuge of sinners, the Comforter of the afflicted.   And ' let the first amongst the king's princes walk before her,' let angels and prophets, and apostles, and martyrs, and all saints, kiss the hem of her garment and rejoice under the shadow of her throne.

WEDDĀSÊ MĀRYĀM (between 431 and 451).

And now we will write the praises of our Lady, and Mother of God, the Virgin Mary, to whom prayer and petition shall be offered, by the children of Baptism, world without end.

Thou shalt be named the Beloved One, O thou blessèd among women. Thou art that second Chamber which is called the Holy of Holies. . . .

Thou art the pure chest of gold in which was laid up the manna, that bread which came down from Heaven, and the Giver of life to all the world.

Thou art that candlestick of gold which didst bear the shining Lamp, all times a light to the world. . . .

Thou art that golden censer which bore the coals of blessèd fire, which He who shall forgive us our sins and do away transgression took of thee.

Thou art the sweet-smelling flower that sprang up from the root of Jesse.

The rod of Aaron, that budded though unplanted, and unwatered, such art thou, O Mother of Christ. . . .

Thou art truly the glory of our race, and the petitioner for life to our souls.

Thou art the ladder seen by Jacob which reached from earth to Heaven, and by which the angels of God were ascending and descending.

Thou art the wood which Moses saw in the flame of fire, when the wood was not consumed.

Thou art that field in which seed was not sown, and yet living Fruit came forth from thee.

Thou art the treasure which Joseph purchased, and

THE MADONNA WITH SS. FRANCIS AND LIBERALE

Giorgione

found therein the precious Pearl, Our Saviour Jesus Christ.

Rejoice, O Mother of God, thou joy of Angels.

Rejoice, O pure one, foretold by prophets.

O Virgin, O Holy, O Mother of the Lord. Rightly art thou called, she who hath wondrously borne the King. A mystery abode on thee for our salvation. Let us keep silence, for we cannot express it aright, on account of the dignity of the Benefactor. . . .

Where is the tongue that shall be able to utter what should be said of thee, O Virgin Mother of the Word of the Father ? Thou hast become the throne of the King whom the Cherubim do bear. We will call thee Blessèd, and will remember thy name to all generations, O fair Dove, Mother of Our Lord Jesus Christ. . . .

Great things and marvellous shall they speak concerning thee, O thou City of God ; for thou hast been the dwelling-place of the Word of the Father.

All the kings of the earth shall come to thy light, and the people to thy brightness, O Virgin Mary.

Rejoice, O thou intellectual Garden, wherein Christ the Second Adam made His abode. . . .

Rejoice, O thou pure Star, adorned with all the Beauty of Praise.

Rejoice, O Bush, which the fire of His Deity did not consume.

Let us sanctify Mary as the Mother of God, because in the city of David Our Lord and Saviour Jesus Christ was born of her.

SELWYN IMAGE (1849-).

 Mother of God on high !
We kneel at thy feet, dear Maid and Mother,
Who hast borne us God for our very Brother.

 Mother and Maid ! we lie
Here at thy feet, who cry to thee, love thee,
Praising none but the Lord above thee.

 Mother of God's Own Child !
We who are called by His Name belong to thee,
We, thy children, chanting our song to thee.

 Mother ! the days are wild :
Oh, let those arms and that sweet smile, round us,
Cherish and guard, or our sins confound us.

 Star of the Sea ! we drive
Drenched and drowned, 'mid the waves that deride
  us,
Lost on the rocks, if thou shine not and guide us.

 How may we pass alive
Through the desert world, but with thee, the Rose
  of it ?
By thy fragrance stayed, till the dim, parched close
  of it.

 Vine and Lily and Rose !
In His garden, lo ! thy Beloved sets us ;
Scorn not thou, though the earth forgets us.

THE HOLY FAMILY

Correggio

Lady of Grief ! unclose
Thy stricken soul to our souls that cry to thee,
Stricken of grief, that grief may fly to thee.

Lady of Joys ! though seven
Times seven are the charms of sin to beguile us,
Lost in thy charm, what sin shall defile us ?

Lady and Queen of Heaven !
Here, on earth, we would serve before thee,
In thy very court at last to adore thee.

Mary, Mother and Queen !
Bring us at length, where the angels lean,
Choir on choir, beneath thy grace :
Bring us all to that hidden place,
Where face to face thyself thou art seen,
  O Mary Queen !

BEN JONSON (1573-1637).

Daughter and Mother and the Spouse of God,
 Alike of kin to that most Blessèd Trine
 Of Persons, yet in Union, One, Divine,
How are thy gifts and graces blazed abro'd.

Most holy, and pure Virgin, Blessèd Mayd,
 Sweet Tree of Life, King David's Strength and
  Tower,
 The House of Gold, the Gate of Heaven's power,
The Morning-Star whose light our fall hath stay'd.

Great Queen of Queens, most mild, most meek,
    most wise,
    Most venerable, Cause of all our joy,
    Whose chearful look our sadness doth destroy,
And art the spotless Mirror to man's eyes.

The Seat of Sapience, the most lovely Mother,
    And most to be admired of thy sexe,
    Who mad'st us happy all, in thy reflexe,
By bringing forth God's Onely Son, no other.

Thou Throne of Glory, beauteous as the moone,
    The rosie morning, or the rising sun,
    Who like a giant hastes his course to run,
Till he hath reached his twofold point of noone.

How are thy gifts and graces blazed abro'd,
    Through all the lines of this circumference,
    T'imprint in all purged hearts this Virgin sence
Of being Daughter, Mother, Spouse of God ?

ROBERT HUGH BENSON (1871-1914).

  ' Hail, Mary ! ' Gabriel whispered, as he dropt—
    A shining herald of the Holy Three.
  ' Hail, Mary ! ' and the dying world half-stopt
      His sick, sin-laden breath
      In nestling Nazareth ;
And singing cherubim looked down to see.

  ' Hail, Mary ! ' See, the trembling of the air ;
    The Presence moves about her soft as fire ;

For righteousness and peace have kissèd there.
       And suddenly the Shrine
       Is bright with light Divine,
The Hope of Israel and the world's Desire.

He whom we sought came suddenly, and found
   His Temple clean from every spot of sin ;
And all the world seems consecrated ground ;
       Her prayers, like incense, rise ;
       And see, her very eyes
Shine like twin tapers as the Lord comes in.

Where the four mystic Eden-rivers rise
   The Angel-guard, that stands above the vale
And keeps the gate of sunlit Paradise,
       Let fall his sword of flame
       And cried upon thy name,
' Hail, Mary ! ' and the garden answered ' Hail ! '

Shouted the sons of God ; the morning stars
   Sang once again, as when the Lord began
To build the hills with battlements and bars.
       Ah, what a cry there fell !—
       ' Jesus, Emmanuel,'
The Lord of Angels and the Son of Man !

' Hail, Mary ! ' For the world remembers yet
   The Maiden Mother and the Holy Son ;
Remembers ! How can any child forget
       The hope of heaven and thee—
       Such stainless purity—
Sin conquered, and the reign of peace begun ?

Remembers !   Yea, if I remember not
　　The joys of Nazareth and Bethlehem,
Yet can thy dolours never be forgot :
　　　　Thy thorn-crowned Son and thee
　　　　Set high on Calvary,
The whole world mourns for—and remembers them.

' Hail, Mary ! '   When the ungenerous sons of men
　　Grieve at thy glory, strip thee of thy praise,
The beasts and birds take up the song again
　　　　With carol shrill and high
　　　　Of Maying melody :
' Hail, Mary, Mary Maiden, full of grace ! '

O Mother, take this verse and pray for me,
　　Now and at my last hour, lest that the cost
Of my redemption, and thy charity,
　　　　Be wasted on thy child,
　　　　O Mary undefiled,—
Lest grace be vanquished and a sinner lost !

JOHN LINGARD (1771-1851).

Hail, Queen of Heav'n, the ocean Star !
　　Guide of the wand'rer here below !
Thrown on life's surge, we claim thy care—
　　Save us from peril and from woe.
　　　　Mother of Christ, Star of the sea,
　　　　Pray for the wanderer, pray for me.

THE SISTINE MADONNA

Raphael

O gentle, chaste, and spotless Maid,
    We sinners make our prayers through thee ;
Remind thy Son that He has paid
    The price of our iniquity.
        Virgin most pure, Star of the sea,
        Pray for the sinner, pray for me.

Sojourners in this vale of tears,
    To thee, blest advocate, we cry ;
Pity our sorrows, calm our fears,
    And soothe with hope our misery.
        Refuge in grief, Star of the sea,
        Pray for the mourner, pray for me.

And while to Him who reigns above,
    In Godhead One, in Persons Three,
The Source of life, of grace, of love,
    Homage we pay on bended knee ;
        Do thou, bright Queen, Star of the sea,
        Pray for thy children, pray for me.

THE ROMAN BREVIARY.

Hail, Holy Queen, mother of mercy, Hail, our life,
our sweetness, and our hope. To thee do we cry,
poor banished children of Eve. To thee do we send
up our sighs, mourning, and weeping in this vale of
tears. Turn then, most gracious advocate, thine eyes
of mercy towards us. And after this our exile show
unto us the blessed fruit of thy womb, Jesus. O
clement, O loving, O sweet Virgin Mary.

VIII

AT THE CROSS

Now there stood by the cross of Jesus his mother.—*St. John* xix. 25.

RICHARD CRASHAW (? 1613-1649).

*A pathetical descant upon the devout plain-song of
Stabat Mater Dolorosa.*

In shade of death's sad tree stood doleful she.
Ah, she, now by none other
Name to be known, alas, but Sorrow's Mother.
    Before her eyes,
      Hers, and the whole world's joys,
Hanging all torn she sees ; and in his woes
    And pains, her pangs and throes :
Each wound of his, from every part,
All, more at home in her one heart.

What kind of marble, then, is that cold man
Who can look on and see,
Nor keep such noble sorrows company ?
    Sure, e'en from you
      (My flints) some drops are due,
To see so many unkind swords contest
    So fast for one soft breast ;

CHRIST WITH HIS PARENTS RETURNING FROM THE TEMPLE

Rembrandt

While, with a faithful, mutual flood,
Her eyes bleed tears, his wounds weep blood.

Oh, costly intercourse of deaths, and worse—
Divided loves.   While Son and Mother
Discourse alternate wounds to one another,
 Quick deaths that grow
 And gather, as they come and go.
His nails write swords in her, which soon her heart
 Pays back with more than their own smart.
Her swords, still growing with his pain,
Turn spears, and straight come home again.

She sees her Son, her God, bow with a load
Of borrowed sins ; and swim
In woes that were not made for him.
 Ah, hard command
 Of love ; here must she stand,
Charged to look on, and with a steadfast eye
 See her Life die ;
Leaving her only so much breath
As serves to keep alive her death.

O Mother, Turtle-dove, soft Source of Love,
That these dry lids might borrow
Something from thy full seas of sorrow.
 Oh, in that breast
 Of thine—the noblest nest
Both of love's fires and floods—might I recline
 This hard, cold heart of mine.
The chill lump would relent, and prove
Soft subject for the siege of love.

P

Oh, teach those wounds to bleed in me; me, so to read
This book of loves, thus writ
In lines of death, my life may copy it
　　　With loyal cares.
　　　Oh, let me here claim shares.
Yield something in thy sad prerogative
　　　(Great Queen of Griefs), and give
Me, too, my tears ; who, though all stone,
Think much that thou shouldst mourn alone.

Yea, let my life and me fix here with thee,
And at the humble foot
Of this fair tree take our eternal root.
　　　That so we may
　　　At least be in love's way ;
And in these chaste wars, while the winged wounds
　　flee
　　　So fast 'twixt him and thee,
My breast may catch the kiss of some kind dart,
Though, as at second hand, from either heart.

O you, your own best darts, dear, doleful hearts,
Hail, and strike home, and make me see
That wounded bosoms their own weapons be.
　　　Come, wounds ; come, darts ;
　　　Nailed hands and piercèd hearts ;
Come, your whole selves, Sorrow's great Son and
　　Mother ;
　　　Nor grudge a younger brother
Of griefs his portion, who (had all their due)
One single wound should not have left for you.

CHRIST TAKING LEAVE OF HIS MOTHER

Albert Dürer

Shall I set there so deep a share
(Dear wounds), and only now
In sorrows draw no dividend with you ?
  Oh, be more wise,
  If not more soft, mine eyes ;
Flow, tardy founts, and into decent showers
  Dissolve my days and hours :
And, if thou yet (faint soul) desert
To bleed with him, fail not to weep with her.

Rich Queen, lend some relief ; at least an alms of
 grief
To a heart who, by sad right of sin,
Could prove the whole sum (too sure) due to him.
  By all those stings
  Of love, sweet-bitter things,
Which these torn hands transcribed on thy true
 heart ;
  Oh, teach mine, too, the art
To study him so, till we mix
Wounds, and become one crucifix.

Oh, let me suck the wine so long of this chaste Vine,
Till, drunk of the dear wounds, I be
A lost thing to the world, as it to me.
  O faithful Friend
  Of me and of my end,
Fold up my life in love ; and lay it beneath
  My dear Lord's vital death.
Lo, heart, thy hope's whole plea, her precious breath
Poured out in prayers for thee—thy Lord's in death.

JOHN TAULER (1300-1361).

There stood also by the Cross of Jesus his most holy and ever-virgin Mother Mary. . . .

And how couldst thou stand ?   Whence came thy strength ?   Of a certainty, thy body was not of steel or stone, that this day thou couldst be pierced so many times by the sword of sorrow, and crucified so many times, and wounded together with thy Son, nevertheless thou didst stand there firm both in body and soul. Peradventure those strong and rough nails held thee also fast upon the Cross of thy Son, so that thou couldst not fall.   But far more strongly did thy mighty love, love stronger than death itself, bear thee up, so that thou couldst not fall.   Thou stoodest, therefore, the immovable column of the faith. . . .

Therefore thou stoodest by his Cross, and didst adore his Godhead in spirit.   Truly thou stoodest like some strong tower, in which the king, who had set forth on a long journey, had hidden the precious treasure of faith.   And, because all grief and compassion that spring from love are great according to the measure of love, therefore, because thy love was beyond all measure, thy grief was utterly measureless. And because thou knewest Jesus, thy beloved Son, to be the true Son of God, thy love for his Godhead, and thy love for his Manhood, like two mighty rocks, pressed together thy heart between them, and straitened it in mortal agony, when thou sawest Jesus, the Son of God, treated so horribly and shamefully in his human nature, and so cruelly put to death.   Of a truth, these were the two sharp swords that cruelly pierced thy soul with all affliction and grief. For, as a bride full of burning love, thou hadst bitter grief for the grievous contempt and wrong which thou sawest inflicted on thy Bridegroom, even thy God and Lord, and, as a faithful and true Mother, thou didst sorrow exceedingly. Moreover, because the Passion of this thy Son was so exceeding great, that according to the rigour of justice it might outweigh by its own weight all the sins of the world, which are numberless and boundless, therefore was thy suffering also measureless and boundless ; and because thy sorrow corresponded with his torments, on that account was thy cross and affliction beyond all comprehension and measure, and thy merits limitless.

JULIAN OF NORWICH (1343-1413).

With cheer of mirth and joy our good Lord looked down on the right side, and brought to my mind where our Lady stood in the time of His Passion, and said : ' Wilt thou see her ? ' And in this sweet word (it was) as if He had said : ' I wot that thou wouldst see My blessèd Mother : for after Myself she is the highest joy that I might shew thee, the most pleasance and worship of Me, and most she is desired to be seen of My blessed creatures.' And for the high marvellous, singular love, that He hath to this sweet Maiden, His blessèd Mother, our Lady Saint Mary, He shewed her highly rejoicing, as by meaning of these words : as if He said : ' Wilt thou see how I love her, that thou mightest joy with Me in the love that I have in her and she in Me ? ' . . . And Jesus . . . shewed me ghostly sight of her: right as I had seen her before, little and simple, as He shewed her high and noble and glorious and pleasing to Him above all creatures.

F. W. FABER (1814-1863).

His Mother cannot reach His face ;
    She stands in helplessness beside ;
Her heart is martyred with her Son's ;
    Jesus, our Love, is crucified.

FRANCIS THOMPSON (1860-1907).

O Lady Mary, thy bright crown
    Is no mere crown of majesty ;
For, with the reflex of his own
    Resplendent thorns Christ circled thee.

The red rose of this Passion-tide
    Doth take a deeper hue from thee,
In the five wounds of Jesus dyed,
    And in thy bleeding thoughts, Mary !

The soldier struck a triple stroke
    That smote thy Jesus on the tree ;
He broke the Heart of hearts, and broke
    The Saint's and Mother's hearts in thee.

CHRIST TAKING LEAVE OF HIS MOTHER
Correggio

Thy Son went up the angels' ways,
  His passion ended ; but, ah me !
Thou found'st the road of further days
  A longer way of Calvary.

On the hard cross of hope deferred,
  Thou hung'st in loving agony,
Until the mortal-dreaded word
  Which chills our mirth, spake mirth to thee.

The angel Death from this cold tomb
  Of life, did roll the stone away ;
And he thou barest in thy womb
  Caught thee at last into the day—
Before the living throne of whom
  The lights of heaven burning pray.

O thou, who dwellest in the day,
  Behold, I pace amidst the gloom :
Darkness is ever round my way
  With little space for sunbeam-room.

Yet, Christian sadness is divine,
  Even as thy patient sadness was :
The salt tears in our life's dark wine
  Fell in it from the saving cross.

Bitter the bread of our repast ;
  Yet, doth a sweet the bitter leaven :
Our sorrow is the shadow cast
  Around it by the light of heaven.

O Light in light, shine down from heaven.

W. Chatterton Dix (1837-1898).

> Mother disconsolate,
> Silent with thee we wait,
>   Watching the end ;
> How shall we mourn with thee
> Him, Who on Calvary
>   Dies, our best Friend ?
>
> How shall we love with thee
> Him, Who to set us free
>   Meekly is bound ?
> How, with thee, calm abide
> Where, from His piercèd side,
>   Blood stains the ground ?
>
> How shall we watch thee bear
> Sorrows He bids thee share,—
>   Son's strangest gift ?
> How feel the sword with thee,
> How in this agony
>   Eyes to Him lift ?
>
> How shall we bear with thee
> Words, from the cruel tree,
>   Lips Divine speak ?
> How with thee take our place,
> Spotless and full of grace,
>   We, sinful, weak ?

THE PROCESSION TO CALVARY

Fra Angelico

Woman, behold thy Son,
Jesus the Holy One,
  Bloodstained and faint !
How can we restless be,
When, Lady, thou and He
  Make no complaint ?

O be it ours to know
Some of thy bitter woe,
  Some of thy bliss :
Some it can only be,
We are so unlike thee,—
  Christ grant us this !

JACOPONE DA TODI (1228-1306).

By the Cross, with grief o'erladen,
Weeping, stood the Mother-Maiden,
  Where her Son hung high in air :
Yea ! her very soul was riven
By the sword of sorrow, driven
  Through the wounds already there.

Oh ! beneath what sore affliction
Bent that child of benediction,
  Mother of God's only Son :
Tender Mother ! how she sorrowed,
As her gaze each moment borrowed
  Anguish from her peerless One.

Q

Who is there his grief could smother,
If he saw Christ's holy Mother
　　Under such a weight of woe ?
Nay, his state were past believing
Who, unmoved, could see her grieving
　　That her Son was suffering so.

For the sins of men, His nation,
Jesus, by His flagellation
　　Agonized, she saw aghast :
Saw her sweet Son God-forsaken,
Though, ere life's last breath was taken,
　　His abandonment had passed.

Mother, fount of love so tender,
Let thy woe so vast engender
　　Woe in me, with thine to grieve :
Make me, loving Christ, so love Him
That now, setting naught above Him,
　　To His will my will may cleave.

Mother mine ! this favour do me :
Drive His dear wounds through and through me ;
　　My heart, too, be crucified :
Since He deigns that all the merit
Of His wounds I should inherit,
　　All His pain with me divide.

Make me thy co-mourner truly,
For His crucifixion duly
　　Sorrowing till my life is o'er :

THE CRUCIFIXION

Antonello da Messina

'Neath the Cross, let my position
Be by thee, and my contrition
   Join thy sorrow evermore.

Virgin of all virgins, Mary,
Be not wroth with me, nor chary
   Of the grief that mine should be :
Let me, mindful of His Passion,
Die in Christ, and, in some fashion,
   Bear the wounds He bore for me.

Let those wounds, reincarnated,
Live in me, inebriated
   With His Cross, His Blood, for aye :
Lest in penal flames I perish,
Hold me, Mother mine, and cherish,
   'Gainst the dreadful Judgment-day.

Christ, my Lord, in life's last hour
Grant me, through Thy Mother's power,
   Even victory's palm to win :
When my soul and body sever,
Grant me Paradise for ever,
   To Thy glory entering in.

ELIZABETH BARRETT BROWNING (1806-1861).

   O Lady of the Passion, dost thou weep ?
   What help can we, then, through our tears survey,
   If such as thou a cause for wailing keep ?
   What help, what hope, for us, sweet Lady, say ?

' Good man, it doth befit thine heart to lay
More courage next it, having seen me so.
All other hearts find other balm to-day—
The whole world's consolation is my woe.'

BISHOP ULLATHORNE (1806-1889).

It was at the foot of the Cross that her Son specially
proclaimed her our Mother ; and this for two reasons :
—that she might have a true experience of the deepest
sorrows of motherhood, so as to sympathise with us ;
and that we might know how only through courageously
and lovingly suffering what God wills, and taking up
our cross as He has commanded, can we ever be her
genuine children. And—to finish my subject with
a suggestion far above ordinary human ideas—this
is not all. We may do more than be worthy and
trustful children of Mary, by doing the Will of God
in all things and loving the Cross. We may even—
O wonderful thought !—share in some sort the
glorious privilege of her Maternity. If this sounds
impossible or presumptuous, listen to Christ Himself ;
for does He not say : ' He who doeth the Will of My
Father Who is in Heaven, the same is My brother, and
My sister, and My Mother.'

ASCRIBED TO THE SERVITE, CALLISTO PALUMBELLA.

Oh ! on what a sea of sorrow
    Was the Virgin-Mother cast,
When her eyes with tears o'erflowing
    Gazed upon her Son aghast,

From the blood-stained gibbet taken,
  Dying in her arms at last.

In her bitter desolation,
  His sweet mouth, His bosom too,
Then His riven side belovèd,
  Then each hand, both wounded through,
Then His feet, with Blood encrimsoned,
  Her maternal tears bedew.

She, a hundred times and over,
  Strains Him closely to her breast
Heart to Heart, arms arms enfolding,
  Are His wounds on her impressed :
Thus, in sorrow's very kisses,
  Melts her anguished soul to rest.

Oh, dear Mother ! we beseech thee,
  By the tears thine eyes have shed,
By the cruel death of Jesus
  And His wounds' right royal red,
Make our hearts o'erflow with sorrow
  From thy heart's deep fountain-head.

To the Father, Son, and Spirit,
  Now we bend an equal knee :
Glory, sempiternal glory,
  To the Most High Trinity ;
Yea ! perpetual praise and honour
  Now and through all ages be.

IX

THE SECOND EVE

He shall save his people from their sins.—*St. Matthew* i. 21.

The Mirror of Our Lady (1430).

Ave Maria. This salutation is taken of the Gospel of the Greeting of the Angel Gabriel and of Elizabeth, and it was the beginning of our health. And therefore this word AVE spelled backward is EVA, for like as Eve talking with the fiend was the beginning of our perdition, so Our Lady's talking with the Angel when he greeted her with this AVE was the entry of our redemption. And so EVA is turned into AVE, for our sorrow is turned into joy by means of Our Lady. For EVA is as much as to say woe, and AVE is as much as to say joy, or without woe. Therefore, meekly and reverently thanking this glorious Queen of Heaven, and Mother of Our Saviour, for our deliverance, say we devoutely to her AVE MARIA, Hail Mary.

Robert Southwell (1560-1595).

Spell Eva back and Ave shall you find ;
The first began, the last reversed our harms :
An angel's witching words did Eva blind ;
An angel's Ave disenchants the charms :

126

THE VIRGIN AT THE CRUCIFIXION

M. Grünewald

Death first by woman's weakness entered in ;
In Woman's virtue life doth now begin.

O Virgin-breast, the heavens to thee incline
In thee their joy and sovereign they agnize ;
Too mean their glory is to match with thine,
Whose chaste receipt God more than heaven did
    prize.
Hail, fairest Heaven, that heaven and earth dost
    bless,
Where virtues' stars, God's sun of justice is.

With haughty mind to Godhead man aspired,
And was by pride from place of pleasure chased ;
With loving mind our manhead God desired,
And us by love in greater pleasure placed :
Man labouring to ascend procured our fall ;
God yielding to descend cut off our thrall.

RICHARD CRASHAW (? 1613-1649).

Hail, most high, most humble one !
Above the world, below thy Son,
Whose blush the moon beauteously mars
And stains the timorous light of stars.
He that made all things had not done
Till He had made Himself thy Son.
The whole world's Host would be thy guest,
And board Himself at thy rich breast.
O boundless hospitality,
The Feast of all things feeds on thee !

The first Eve, mother of our fall,
Ere she bore any one slew all.
Of her unkind gift might we have
The inheritance of a hasty grave ;
Quick buried in the wanton tomb
   Of one forbidden bit,
Had not a Better Fruit forbidden it ;
   Had not thy healthful womb
The world's new Eastern window been,
And given us Heav'n again in giving Him,
Thine was the rosy dawn that sprung the day
Which renders all the stars she stole away.
   Let then the aged world be wise, and all
Prove nobly, here, unnatural :
   'Tis gratitude to forget that other,
And call the Maiden Eve their Mother.
   Ye redeemed nations far and near,
Applaud your happy selves in her,
(All you to whom this love belongs)
And keep't alive with lasting songs.
   Let hearts and lips speak loud and say,
Hail, Door of Life, and Source of Day !
The door was shut, the fountain sealed,
Yet light was seen and life revealed ;
The fountain sealed, yet life found way.
   Glory to Thee, great Virgin's Son,
In bosom of Thy Father's bliss !
The same to Thee, sweet Spirit, be done,
As ever shall be, was and is !

THE VIRGIN AT THE CRUCIFIXION

Perugino

St. Ephrem (Fourth Century).

Prophets all, rejoice in Mary ;
For in her your songs are ended,
All your prophecies are perfect,
All your words are proved and strengthened.
Patriarchs all, rejoice in Mary ;
See, she takes your promised blessing,
In her Son she makes you perfect—
Priests and saints and seers he hallows.
For the bitter fruit our mother
Plucked from off the tree of knowledge,
See, the sweet Fruit Mary gives us,
Wherewith all the world is sweetened.
Now, the Tree of Life, once hidden
In the midst of Eden's garden,
Grows in Mary, springeth from her,
Far and wide its sweet fruits sending ;
And the whole creation resteth
In the shadow of its branches.
Mary weaves the robe of glory,
Gives it to her father Adam,
Who mid Eden's trees was naked,
Clothing him with peace and beauty.
Whom the wife o'erthrew, the Daughter
Lifteth, and his heart is gladdened.
Eve and Satan leagued together
Dug the pit for Adam's ruin.
Mary with the angel speaketh,
And from out the deep they lift him,

R

By the mystery, hid for ages,
Come to light for Adam's healing.
Now the Virgin-Vine hath borne us
Grapes, that make the wine of sweetness,
Where our parents, Eve and Adam,
Find true comfort in their sorrow,
Taste the drink of life and healing,
And their woes are lost in gladness.

ST. VENANTIUS FORTUNATUS (Sixth Century).

Hail, thou Star of Ocean,
    Portal of the sky,
Ever-Virgin Mother
    Of the Lord Most High.

Oh, by Gabriel's Ave
    Uttered long ago,
Eva's name reversing,
    'Stablish peace below.

Break the captive's fetters,
    Light on blindness pour,
All our ills expelling,
    Every bliss implore.

Show thyself a Mother,
    Offer Him our sighs,
Who for us Incarnate,
    Did not thee despise.

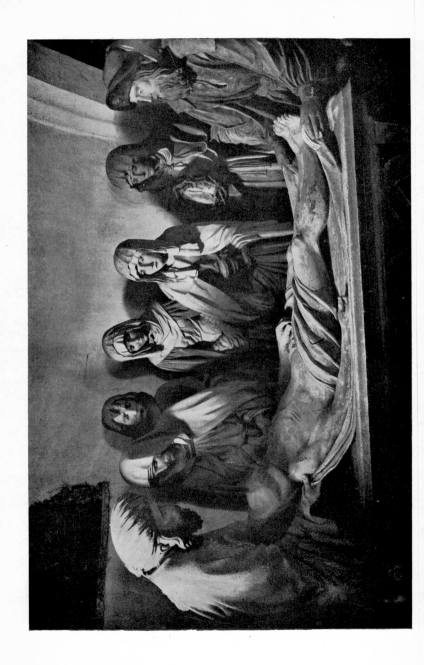

Virgin of all virgins,
    To thy shelter take us :
Gentlest of the gentle,
    Chaste and gentle make us.

Still as on we journey,
    Help our weak endeavour
Till with thee and Jesus
    We rejoice for ever.

DANTE (1265-1321).

Parent of virtue, Light eternal, thou
    Of whom was born the meek benignant Fruit
    That suffered on the cross a bitter death,
    To save us sinners from the dark abyss :
Thou, Queen of Heaven supreme, and of this
      world,
    Vouchsafe to entreat thy meritorious Son
    To lead me to his heavenly kingdom's joys,
    Through guidance of his never-failing grace.
Thou know'st my hope was ever placed in thee ;
    In thee, thou know'st, was still my sole delight ;
    O Goodness infinite, assist me now :
Help me, for at the bourne I am arrived
    Which I must soon inevitably pass ;
    My Comforter, oh, now desert me not.
For every fault committed here on earth
My soul deplores, and contrite is my heart.

St. John Chrysostom (347-407).

A virgin cast us forth from paradise ; through a Virgin we have found eternal life. By what things we were condemned, by these same are we cured. . . . By what things the devil worsted us, by these same did Christ overcome him. He took those same arms, and with them He prostrated him. And how ? Listen. A virgin, wood, and death were the symbols of our defeat. For Eve was a virgin ; the wood was the tree ; death was the punishment pronounced on Adam. Thou seest how a virgin, wood, and death were the symbols of our defeat. Now see how these very same are the cause of our victory. Instead of Eve, Mary. Instead of the tree of knowledge of good and evil, the wood of the Cross. Instead of Adam's death, the Lord's Death.

Coventry Patmore (1823-1896).

In season due, on His sweet-fearful bed,
Rock'd by an earthquake, curtain'd with eclipse,
Thou shar'd'st the rapture of the sharp spear's head,
And thy bliss pale
Wrought for our boon what Eve's did for our bale ;
Thereafter, holding a little thy soft breath,
Thou underwent'st the ceremony of death ;
And, now, Queen-Wife,
Sitt'st at the right hand of the Lord of Life,

Who, of all bounty, craves for only fee
The glory of hearing it besought with smiles by
thee !
Ora pro me !

ASCRIBED TO HERMANNUS CONTRACTUS (1013-1054).

Hail ! thou Queen, and mercy's Mother,
Life, and sweetness like none other ;
Hail ! our hope : on thee we call,
Eva's banished children all.

From this vale of tears we send thee
Sighs, and moans, and tears, to bend thee ;
On us, Advocate divine,
Turn those pitying eyes of thine.

Virgin Mary, sweet and pious,
And too clement to deny us,
Show us, when our exile 's done,
Jesus, thy own blessèd Son.

X

THE ASSUMPTION AND CORONATION

And there appeared a great sign in heaven ; a woman clothed with the sun, . . . and upon her head a crown of twelve stars.—*Rev.* xii. 1.

RICHARD CRASHAW (? 1613-1649).

Hark ; she is called, the parting hour is come ;
Take thy farewell, poor world, Heaven must go
  home.
A piece of heavenly-earth ; purer and brighter
Than the chaste stars, whose choice lamps come to
  light her,
Whilst through the crystal orbs clearer than they
She climbs ; and makes a far more milky-way.
She 's called.   Hark, how the dear immortal Dove
Sighs to his silver Mate, ' Rise up, my Love ;
Rise up, my Fair, my spotless One ' :
The winter 's past ; the rain is gone ;
The spring is come ; the flowers appear—
No sweets (save thou) are wanting here.
Come away, my Love ; come away, my Dove ;
          Cast off delay :
The court of heaven is come to wait upon thee home;
          Come, come away.
          The flowers appear,
Or quickly would, wert thou once here.

THE ENTOMBMENT
Caravaggio

The spring is come, or, if it stay,
'Tis to keep time with thy delay.
The rain is gone, except so much as we
Detain in needful tears, to weep the want of thee.
      The winter is past,
        Or, if he make less haste,
His answer is, why she does so,
If summer come not, how can winter go ?
      Come away, come away.
The shrill winds chide ; the waters weep thy stay ;
The fountains murmur ; and each loftiest tree
Bows lowest his leafy top, to look for thee.
Come away, my Love ; come away, my Dove ;
      Cast off delay :
The court of heaven is come to wait upon thee home ;
      Come, come away.

    She's called again.   And will she go ?
    When heaven bids come, who can say No ?
    Heaven calls her, and she must away ;
    Heaven will not, and she cannot, stay.
    Go, then ; go, glorious on the golden wings
    Of the bright youth of heaven, that sings
    Under so sweet a burden.   Go,
    Since thy dread Son will have it so.
    And while thou goest, our song and we
    Will, as we may, reach after thee.
    Hail, holy Queen of humble hearts :
    We, in thy praise, will have our parts.
And though thy dearest looks must now give light
To none but the blest heavens, whose bright

Beholders, lost in sweet delight,
Feed for ever their fair sight
With those divinest eyes, which we
And our dark world no more shall see ;
Though our poor eyes are parted so,
Yet shall our lips never let go
Thy gracious name ; but, to the last,
Our loving song shall hold it fast.

    Thy precious name shall be
    Thyself to us ; and we
    With holy care will keep it by us.
    We to the last will hold it fast,
    And no Assumption shall deny us.
    All the sweetest showers
    Of our fairest flowers
    Will we strew upon it.
    Though our sweets cannot make
    It sweeter, they can take
    Themselves new sweetness from it.

Maria, men and angels sing,
Maria, Mother of our King.
Live, rosy Princess, live ; and may the bright
Crown of a most incomparable light
Embrace thy radiant brows.   Oh, may the best
Of everlasting joys bathe thy white breast.
Live, our chaste Love, the holy Mirth
Of heaven, the humble Pride of earth.
Live, Crown of women, Queen of men ;
Live, Mistress of our song.   And when
Our weak desires have done their best,
Sweet angels come and sing the rest.

Francis Thompson (1860-1907).

' Mortals, that behold a Woman
   Rising 'twixt the Moon and Sun ;
Who am I the heavens assume ? an
   All am I, and I am one.

' Multitudinous ascend I,
   Dreadful as a battle arrayed,
For I bear you whither tend I ;
   Ye are I : be undismayed !
I, the Ark that for the graven
   Tables of the Law was made ;
Man's own heart was one ; one, Heaven ;
   Both within my womb were laid.
For there Anteros with Eros,
   Heaven with man, conjoinèd was,—
Twin-stone of the Law, Ischyros,
   Agios Athanatos.

' I, the flesh-girt Paradises
   Gardened by the Adam new,
Daintied o'er with dear devices
   Which He loveth, for He grew.
I, the boundless strict savannah
   Which God's leaping feet go through ;
I, the heaven whence the Manna,
   Weary Israel, slid on you !
He the Anteros and Eros,
   I the body, He the Cross ;
He upbeareth me, Ischyros,
   Agios Athanatos !

s

' I am Daniel's mystic Mountain,
  Whence the mighty stone was rolled ;
I am the four Rivers' Fountain,
  Watering Paradise of old ;
Cloud down-raining the Just One am,
  Danae of the Shower of Gold ;
I the Hostel of the Sun am ;
  He the Lamb, and I the Fold.
He the Anteros and Eros,
  I the body, He the Cross ;
He is fast to me, Ischyros,
  Agios Athanatos !

' I, the presence-hall where Angels
  Do enwheel their placèd King—
Even my thoughts which, without change else,
  Cyclic burn and cyclic sing.
To the hollow of Heaven transplanted,
  I a breathing Eden spring,
Where with venom all outpanted
  Lies the slimed Curse shrivelling.
For the brazen Serpent clear on
  That old fangèd knowledge shone ;
I to Wisdom rise, Ischyron,
  Agion Athanaton !

' Then commanded and spake to me
  He who framed all things that be ;
And my Maker entered through me,
  In my tent His rest took He.
Lo ! He standeth, Spouse and Brother,
  I to Him, and He to me,

MOURNING OVER THE DEAD CHRIST

Buonconsiglio

Who upraised me where my mother
  Fell, beneath the apple-tree.
Risen 'twixt Anteros and Eros,
  Blood and Water, Moon and Sun,
He upbears me, He Ischyros,
  I bear Him, the Athanaton ! '

Where is laid the Lord arisen ?
  In the light we walk in gloom ;
Though the Sun has burst his prison,
  We know not his biding-room.
Tell us where the Lord sojourneth,
  For we find an empty tomb.
' Whence He sprung, there He returneth,
  Mystic Sun—the Virgin's Womb.'
Hidden Sun, His beams so near us,
  Cloud enpillared as He was
From of old, there He, Ischyros,
  Waits our search, Athanatos.

' Who will give Him me for brother,
  Counted of my family,
Sucking the sweet breasts of my Mother ?—
  I His flesh, and mine is He ;
To my Bread myself the bread is,
  And my Wine doth drink me : see,
His left hand beneath my head is,
  His right hand embraceth me !
Sweetest Anteros and Eros,'
  Lo, her arms He leans across ;
Dead that we die not, stooped to rear us,
  Thanatos Athanatos.

Who is She, in candid vesture,
  Rushing up from out the brine ?
Treading with resilient gesture
  Air, and with that Cup divine ?
She in us and we in her are,
  Beating Godward ; all that pine,
Lo, a wonder and a terror—
  The Sun hath blushed the Sea to Wine !
He the Anteros and Eros,
  She the Bride and Spirit ; for
Now the days of promise near us,
  And the Sea shall be no more.

Open wide thy gates, O Virgin,
  That the King may enter thee !
At all gates the clangours gurge in,
  God's paludament lightens, see !
Camp of Angels !   Well we even
  Of this thing may doubtful be,—
If thou art assumed to Heaven,
  Or is Heaven assumed to thee !
Consummatum.   Christ the promised,
  Thy maiden realm, is won, O Strong !
Since to such sweet Kingdom comest,
  Remember me, poor Thief of Song !

Cadent falls the stars along :—
  ' Mortals, that behold a Woman
    Rising 'twixt the Moon and Sun ;
  Who am I the heavens assume ? an
    All am I, and I am one.'

J. B. Tabb (1845-1909).

> Behold ! the mother bird
> The Fledgeling's voice hath heard !
> He calls anew,
> ' It was thy breast
> That warmed the nest
> From whence I flew.
> Upon a loftier tree
> Of life I wait for thee ;
> Rise, mother-dove, and come,
> Thy Fledgeling calls thee home ! '

Katherine Tynan.

The Father saith, ' Welcome, my Daughter ' :
    Saith the Spirit, ' Welcome, my Spouse ' :
What have angels and archangels brought her ?
    Stars for her brows.

' Welcome, Mother,' the Son saith only,
    ' Welcome, Mother.' The years were slow
While she waited—the years were lonely—
    The summons to go.

Twelve long years of winter and summer,
    Feeding patient his altar-light,
Michael tarried—the lordly comer
    Whose torch was bright.

Now, the Three in Unity claim her
    Close to each in the tenderest bond ;
Now, the Three in Unity name her
    Holy and fond.

Now, the angels float from the azure,
　　Kiss her feet and her mantle's rim ;
She looks up at her Son, her Treasure,
　　Hungry for Him.

Little feet that were wont to falter,
　　Little fingers her lips once kissed :
Ages, spaces, His will can alter,
　　Yea, as He list.

Mother of Christ, and all men's Mother,
　　Where thou sittest the stars between,
Pluck His robe for His toiling brother
　　Stricken with sin.

Yea, the strong desire of His Passion :
　　Yea, the fruit of His mortal pain—
Intercede for thy mournful nation,
　　Mother of men.

Intercede for thy mournful nation
　　Toiling, stricken, seething beneath—
Yea, the strong desire of His Passion
　　Bought with His Death.

ROBERT SOUTHWELL (1560-1595).

If sin be captive, grace must find release ;
　　From curse of sin the innocent is free ;
Tomb, prison is for sinners that decease ;
　　No tomb, but throne to guiltless doth agree :

THE VIRGIN AND THE DEAD CHRIST
Michelangelo

Though thralls of sin lie lingering in their grave,
Yet, faultless corpse, with soul, reward must
    have.

The dazzled eye doth dimmèd light require,
    And dying sights repose in shrouding shades ;
But, eagles' eyes to brightest light aspire,
    And living look delight in lofty glades :
        Faint-wingèd fowl by ground doth faintly fly,
        Our princely Eagle mounts unto the sky.

Gem to her worth, Spouse to her Love ascends,
    Prince to her throne, Queen to her heavenly King,
Whose court with solemn pomp on her attends,
    And choirs of saints with greeting notes do sing :
        Earth rend'reth up her undeservèd prey ;
        Heaven claims the right, and bears the prize
        away.

St. Venantius Fortunatus (Sixth Century).

Next to Him born of thee, the Eternal King,
Enthroned thou art as Queen, O Mother rich,
E'en by thy child-birth wealthily adorned.
Lo, come the Chiefs.   First in great glory, John,
To God foreknown, ere suffered He as man.
And then with Paul, and all his brethren blest,
Peter, their prince and doctor, shining palm :
Clad all in purest gold, more bright than stars—
If thus disciples, what must the Mother be ?
See here the patriarchs and prophets join,
Their gifts presenting at thy lofty throne.

Lo there the Martyr cohort girt with crowns ;
Stephen their prince : the civic crowd of heaven.
And there those earliest buds of passion-flower,
The suckling holocaust of Bethlehem,
That earned at birth, by dying, deathless life.
From Rome they come, the world's metropolis ;
From Alexandria, and from Antioch ;
These from Jerusalem, Byzantium ;
From Patra, Ephesus, and Maddaver.
E'en all from East, or West, or South, or North,
Whose bodies buried life in earth or sea ;
Of various race whole nations, armies, kings,
Run to the Father's gifts of marvel new ;
And men from every land of morn or eve,
Arabia, Persia, Thrace, Ind, Britain, meet.
But ere they come, how does that Lover, whom
Thy womb erst bore, array thee, Virgin blest ?
Largely of heaven He gives thee, who to Him
Once wert a straightened home ; in recompense
For thy womb's hospitality, a throne :
Crowns thy fair brow with aureate diadem,
With sparkling gems tricks out thy golden hair,
Circles thy snow-white neck with necklace rare,
Covers thy breasts all-pure with dazzling sheen ;
Such beauteous robe of honour vests thee with,
Its purple dye with burning splendour glows.
Such as no eye hath seen, nor ear heard tell,
Are, holy Virgin, these thy ornaments ;
So that when Heaven, and all its starry hosts
Gaze on thy grace, they raise their voice to praise.
Michael beginning, with his serried troops,

MOURNING OVER THE DEAD CHRIST

Titian

These plaudits offers to thy maiden Name :
' O paragon of beauty, Woman blest,
Salvation's form, potent by child-birth's Fruit,
Pleasing to God through thy virginity :
By thee the world's Redemption to be born
Hath deigned, and thus repair the race of man,
Which cruel Eve by sin had led astray.
This succouring aid, O Mother, due to thee
A thousand thousand legions, through their ranks,
Loudly proclaim with hymn, and voice, and lyre.'
The Bridal Angel next takes up the strain,
Who brought of yore from heaven the holy news :
' O happy one, Virgin inimitable,
Sheep of that Lamb, who the wolf's jaws hath
        crushed :
In bursting Tartarus, thou bringest home
Captives to father-land, and hast restored
Souls, kept in durance vile, to liberty.'
Now all on either side swell forth the praise,
That in full chorus rolls from choir to choir.
Then Earth in turn begins applauses new ;
And Zach'ry's son, voice, trumpet, herald, sound—
With Peter, Stephen, and the leaders all,
Each in his full battalion myriad-fold—
High o'er their mingled lauds, his voice uplifts :
' O peerless Virgin, born for joys of bliss,
Help of the earth, lustre and pride of heaven !
Lo, how thy flowering womb the world hath blest !
Since to thy bringing-forth in faith we owe
That paradise now holds us denizens.
What are we, or what were we rather ?   Those
T

Whom Eve so deep in ruin whelmed ; and thou
Hast in thy bosom borne from the mire to heaven.'
Thus in thy honour, Mother of God, resound
Through all the starry sphere, shouts of applause,
As crashing thunder-claps, or battle's roar.
But I, alas, wishing to add my meed—
For who 'd not fain thy sacred Name extol ?—
Seem from thy praises only to detract.
Who for the Mother would speak worthily,
Let him beseech the Son, for Whose dear love
Thou liv'st henceforth in this thy glory new.
Beyond all gems in beauty, the sun in splendour
    paling,
Raised higher than the heavens, in lustre stars out-
    shining,
More white than snowy fleeces, more ruddy than
    the morning,
Glistening more bright than sunbeam, to thought
    than honey sweeter :
O passing sweet ! Thy cheek of lovelier tint than
    roses—
To spirit's sense more fragrant than all Arabia's
    perfumes.
Kind, debonair, benignant, holy, majestic, beauteous;
Palm-crown, of grace rich altar, of modesty fair
    flower :
Through thee earth's farthest limits have merited
    Salvation,
In thee the universe of heav'n, land, and sea, rejoices.
  To thee this hymn I offer, unworthy though I be,
  Do thou, of all the succour, be pardon's hope to me.

THE ASCENSION

Mantegna

Dante Gabriel Rossetti (1828-1882).

> Mother of the Fair Delight,
> Thou Handmaid perfect in God's sight,
> Now sitting fourth beside the Three,
> Thyself a Woman-trinity—
> Being a Daughter born to God,
> Mother of Christ from stall to rood,
> And Wife unto the Holy Ghost—
> Oh, when our need is uttermost,
> Think that to such as death may strike
> Thou once wert Sister sister-like :
> Thou Headstone of humanity,
> Groundstone of the great mystery,
> Fashioned like us, yet more than we.
>
> Mind'st thou not (when June's heavy breath
> Warmed the long days in Nazareth)
> That eve thou didst go forth to give
> Thy flowers some drink, that they might live
> One faint night more amid the sands ?
> Far off the trees were as pale wands
> Against the fervid sky : the sea
> Sighed further off eternally,
> As human sorrow sighs in sleep.
> Then, suddenly the awe grew deep,
> As of a day to which all days
> Were footsteps in God's secret ways :
> Until a folding sense, like prayer,
> Which is as God is, everywhere,

Gathered about thee ; and a voice
Spake to thee without any noise,
Being of the silence : ' Hail,' it said,
' Thou that art highly favourèd ;
The Lord is with thee here and now ;
Blessèd among all women thou.'

Ah, knew'st thou of the end, when first
That Babe was on thy bosom nursed ?
Or when he tottered round thy knee,
Did thy great sorrow dawn on thee ?
And through his boyhood, year by year
Eating with him the Passover,
Didst thou discern confusedly
That holier sacrament, when he,
The bitter cup about to quaff,
Should break the bread and eat thereof ?
Or came not yet the knowledge, even
Till on some day forecast in heaven
His feet passed through thy door to press
Upon his Father's business ?
Or still was God's high secret kept ?

Nay, but I think the whisper crept
Like growth through childhood.   Work and play
Things common to the course of day,
Awed thee with meanings unfulfilled ;
And all through girlhood, something stilled
Thy senses like the birth of light,
When thou hast trimmed thy lamp at night,

Or washed thy garments in the stream ;
To whose white bed had come the dream,
That He was thine and thou wast His
Who feeds among the field-lilies.
· Oh, solemn shadow of the end
In that wise spirit long contained.
Oh, awful end ; and those unsaid
Long years, when ' It was finishèd.'

Mind'st thou not (when the twilight gone
Left darkness in the house of John),
Between the naked window-bars
That spacious vigil of the stars ?
For thou, a watcher even as they,
Wouldst rise from where, throughout the day,
Thou wroughtest raiment for His poor ;
And, finding the fixed terms endure
Of day and night, which never brought
Sounds of His coming chariot,
Wouldst lift, through cloud-waste unexplored,
Those eyes which said, ' How long, O Lord ? '
Then, that disciple whom He loved,
Well heeding, haply would be moved
To ask thy blessing in His name ;

And that one thought in both, the same
Though silent, then would clasp ye round
To weep together—tears long bound,
Sick tears of patience, dumb and slow.
Yet, ' Surely, I come quickly ' ; so
He said, from life and death gone home.

Amen : even so, Lord Jesus, come.
But oh, what human tongue can speak
That day, when Michael came to break
From the tired spirit, like a veil,
Its covenant with Gabriel
Endured at length unto the end ?
What human thought can apprehend
That mystery of Motherhood,
When thy Beloved at length renewed
The sweet communion severèd—
His left hand underneath thine head,
And His right hand embracing thee ?
Lo, He was thine ; and this is He.

Soul, is it faith, or love, or hope,
That lets me see her standing up
Where the light of the Throne is bright ?
Unto the left, unto the right,
The cherubim, succinct, conjoint,
Float inward to a golden point,
And from between the seraphim
The glory issues for a hymn.
O Mary Mother, be not loth
To listen—thou whom the stars clothe,
Who seest and mayst not be seen.
Hear us, at last, O Mary Queen ;
Into our shadow bend thy face,
Bowing thee from the secret place,
O Mary Virgin, full of grace.

THE DEATH OF THE VIRGIN

Mantegna

SIR JOHN BEAUMONT (1583-1627).

Who is she that ascends so high,
  Next the Heavenly King,
Round about whom Angels fly
  And her praises sing?

Who is she that, adorned with light,
  Makes the sun her robe,
At whose feet the queen of night
  Lays her changing globe?

To that crown direct thine eye,
  Which her head attires;
There thou mayst her name descry
  Writ in starry fires.

This is she in whose pure womb
  Heaven's Prince remained;
Therefore in no earthly tomb
  Can she be contained.

Heaven she was, which held that fire
  Whence the world took light,
And to Heaven doth now aspire,
  Flames with flames to unite.

She that did so clearly shine
  When our day begun,
See how bright her beams decline
  Now she sits with the Sun.

XI

ORA PRO NOBIS

Holy Mary, Mother of God, pray for us sinners, now and
at the hour of our death.   Amen.

POPE LEO XIII. (1810-1903).

I.

Ardet pugna ferox ; Lucifer ipse, videns,
Horrida monstra furens ex Acheronte vomit.
Ocius, alma Parens, ocius affer opem ;
Tu mihi virtutem, robur et adde novum ;
Contere virgineo monstra inimica pede.
Te duce, Virgo, libens aspera bella geram :
Diffugient hostes ; te duce, victor ero.

II.

Auri dulce melos, dicere, Mater, Ave.
Dicere dulce melos, O pia Mater, Ave.
Tu mihi Deliciae, Spes bona, castus Amor ;
Rebus in adversis tu mihi Praesidium.
Si, mens sollicitis icta cupidinibus,
Tristitiae et luctus anxia sentit onus ;
Si, natum aerumnis videris usque premi,
Materno refove Virgo benigna sinu :

152

Et, cum instante aderit morte suprema dies
Lumina fessa manu molliter ipsa tege,
Et fugientem animam tu bona redde Deo.

TRANSLATION.

I.

Now that the war is raging, fierce and fell,
And man's relentless foe, with wrath beholding
The sons of God his palaces enfolding,
Full many a form of terror sends from hell :
Fast though they fly love's battle to repel,
Faster, oh faster, bring thy succours, Mary ;
Kind Mother of my youth, like Michael,
With virgin-foot tread down each adversary ;
Thou give me strength's invincible accession ;
Thou kindle virtue's meekly shining star :
So shall I rise to tyrant-wrong's repression,
And loose the bands of error, near and far :
To the four winds of heaven my foes will flee ;
Beneath thy flag I move to victory.

II.

Hail, Mary, hail ; to hear the word what pleasure :
Hail, Mary, hail ; to sing the strain what rest :
It is the gold of Araby the blest—
O my fair Hope, chaste Love, enchanting Treasure ;
O my sure Guard—when troubles leave not leisure ;
If, as time wanes, my spirit sinks oppressed,

U

Crushed under cares that know not change, nor
    measure,
Thou soothe my sorrows on thy mother-breast :
And oh, when near my time for homeward passing,
And my frail vessel almost sights the land,
And my tired eyes their last of earth are glassing,
Thou gently close them with thy holy hand :
Then, as I tread the vale with staff and rod,
Commend my spirit to the hands of God.

PETRARCH'S ODE (1304-1374).

Virgin, apart from all and singly placed,
    Who, with thy beauties, hast enamoured heaven,
      Whom none precedeth, none hath seconded ;
Thou that to God hast veritably given,
    By holy thoughts and acts devout and chaste,
      A temple in thy fruitful maidenhead ;
      By thee my life to gladness can be led,
If, by my prayer, kind Maid,
Sweet Mary, thou be swayed,
    Where sin abounds, that grace as far may
      spread.
So, on my spirit's bended knees I pray,
    That, tow'rd a better end,
    Thou may'st amend
My misdirected way.

.   .   .   .   .

Virgin, how many tears have I now spent,
    With many a blandishment and many a vow,
      All to my hurt and my incumbrance sore.

Since I was born in Arno's vale till now,
By turns to this and that direction bent,
My life has been but trouble evermore.
Of mortal charms, words, graces, what a
store
Hath cumbered all my mind.
O Virgin, holy and kind,
Delay not, for my last year I may score.
As swift as arrows fly, my days have flown
In wretchedness and sin ;
And I begin
To wait for death alone.

.   .   .   .   .

Virgin, on whom alone my hopes relie,
Who canst and wilt to my sore trouble give
Thy succours, be thou with me to my end.
Regard not me, but by whose grace I live ;
Let not my merit, but that image high
Which in me dwells, a man so mean, commend.
Thou seest me like a rock, from which descend,
O Virgin, idle streams ;
Some Gorgon, or my dreams,
Have shaped me thus ; but, sorrows do thou
send
More soft and holy to this breast outworn.
Make my last years devout
And pure throughout,
Though some were madness-born.

EDGAR ALLAN POE (1809-1849).

At morn, at noon, at twilight dim,
Maria, thou hast heard my hymn :
In joy and woe, in good and ill,
Mother of God, be with me still.
When the hours flew brightly by,
And not a cloud obscured the sky,
My soul, lest it should truant be,
Thy grace did guide to thine and thee.
Now, when storms of fate o'ercast
Darkly my present and my past,
Let my future radiant shine
With sweet hopes of thee and thine.

JACOPONE DA TODI (1228-1306).

O Queen of all courtesy,
To thee I come and I kneel,
My wounded heart to heal,
To thee for succour I pray—

To thee I come and I kneel,
For lo ! I am in despair ;
None other help can heal,
Thou only wilt hear my prayer :
And if I should lose Thy care,
My spirit must waste away.

My heart is wounded more,
Madonna, than tongue can tell ;

Pierced to the very core,
    Rottenness there doth dwell.
  Hasten to make me well !
    How canst Thou say me nay ?

Madonna, so fierce the strain
    Of this my perilous hour,
  Nature is turned to pain,
    So strong is evil's power ;
    Be gracious, O Ivory Tower !
      My anguish touch and allay.

All that I had is spent :
    In nothingness am I drest ;
  Make me Thine instrument,
    Thy servant ransomed and blest :
    He who drank from Thy breast,
      Madonna, the price will pay.

Thy Son, Who loved me first,—
    By His dear love I entreat,
  Madonna, pity my thirst,
    Grant me Thy counsel meet !
    Succour me, Lily most sweet !
      Haste, and do not delay !

(Madonna speaks)—

  Come to Me, son most dear,
    Thy coming is all my pleasure ;
  Ask my help without fear,
    Gladly I give in due measure ;

Yet, for my skill and treasure,
  In suffering must thou pay.

If that thou wouldst be well,
  Spare thy diet must be ;
Conquer thy senses and quell,
  Teach them from peril to flee ;
  Till they be chastened and free,
    Lest nature ruin and slay.

Then take, for a healing draught,
  Fear of the coming of death :
Though youth both sported and laughed,
  That coming still hasteneth :
  Let vanity, like a breath,
    Fade from its ancient sway.

Then, for a potion, drink
  The solemn terror of Hell :
In that dark prison, O think !
  Lost souls for ever must dwell.
  So, surely, thy heart will swell,
    And cast the poison away !

Before my priest without fear,
  Void forth the Venomous thing :
It is his office to hear,
  And God the ransom will bring !
  So the Enemy's triumphing
    Shall be hushed for ever and aye.

ARTHUR SHEARLY CRIPPS (1869-).

> In that war with no discharge,
> Come, our Mother dear,
> For some that die are motherless,
> Some have no mother near !
> Thy Child He 'll have us ' brethren Mine,'
> So all that die are sons of thine,
> Then bend to all thine ear !
> Smoothe the pillow, kiss the brow—
> Prepare us then,
> Prepare us now—
> That feet be clean, that eyes be clear,
> In that black path to outface the fear—
> Pray for us men !

E. NESBIT (1859-1924).

> The days, the doubts, the dreams of pain
> Are over, not to come again,
> And from the menace of the night
> Has dawned the day-star of delight ;
> My baby lies against me pressed—
> Thus, Mother of God, are mothers blessed !
>
> His little head upon my arm,
> His little body soft and warm,
> His little feet that cannot stand
> Held in the heart of this my hand,
> His little mouth close on my breast—
> Thus, Mary's Son, are mothers blessed.

All dreams of deeds, all deeds of day
Are very faint and far away,
Yet you some day will stand upright
And fight God's foes, in manhood's might,
You—tiny, worshipped, clasped, caressed—
Thus, Mother of God, are mothers blessed.

Whatever grief may come to be
This hour divine goes on for me.
All glorious is my little span,
Since I, like God, have made a man,
A little image of God's best—
Thus, Mary's Son, are mothers blessed.

Come change, come loss, come worlds of tears,
Come endless chain of empty years ;
They cannot take away the hour
That gives me You—my bird, my flower !
Thank God for this !   Leave God the rest !—
Thus, Mother of God, are mothers blessed.

ST. ALPHONSUS MARIA DE LIGUORI (1696-1787).

Mary, thou art Hope the brightest,
    Love most pure and sweet ;
Life and peace I find, reposing
    At thy blessèd feet.
When I call on thee, O Mary,
    When I think on thee,
Joy and pleasure all-entrancing
    Fill my heart with glee.

THE ASSUMPTION OF THE VIRGIN

Titian

If anon the clouds of sadness
    Rise within my heart,
When they hear thy name, O Mary,
    Quickly they depart ;
Like a star on life's dark ocean
    Shining o'er the wave,
Thou canst guide my bark to harbour,
    Thou my soul canst save.
Under thy protecting mantle,
    Queen beloved, I fly ;
There, I wish to live securely ;
    There, I hope to die.
When I come my life to finish,
    Mary, loving thee,
Then, I also know, dear Lady,
    Heaven is gained for me.
Cast thy gentle bonds around me,
    And my heart enchain,
Prisoner of love for ever
    Safe will I remain.
Thus, my heart, O sweetest Mary,
    Is not mine, but thine :
Take it ; give it all to Jesus ;
    Ne'er shall it be mine.

H. N. Oxenham (1829-1888).

Hail, Mary, hail ! the western sky is glowing,
    The sun sinks down 'neath yon empurpled hill,
From distant shores the fresh sea-breeze is blowing,
    Sweet falls the music of the plashing rill.

x

Hail, Mary, hail ! that solemn stillness breaking,
  Sure on the ear a sweeter music fell,
The distant echoes of the valley waking ;
  Hark ! 'tis the summons of the vesper-bell.

Hail, Mary, hail ! like words from the departed
  Speaks the monition of that saint-bell's toll,—
Of blessings slighted to the thankless-hearted,
  Of peace and gladness to the earth-wearied
    soul.

Hail, Mary, hail ! the heavens are faintly lighted,
  The sun is down, the flickering star-beams shine
Pale through the mist-wreaths, while on eyes be-
    nighted
  Streams a mild radiance from the tapered shrine.

Hail, Mary, hail ! the bell hath ceased its ringing,
  The wearied labourer sinks to early rest.
But hark ! within the choir is sweetly singing
  Of Him Who lay, dear Mother, on thy breast.

Hail, Jesus, hail ! to Thee our nightly greetings
  Wakeful we raise, though men around us
    sleep ;
Thou wilt not chide Thy Church's oft repeatings ;
  Do Thou our souls from works of darkness
    keep !

J. C. F. Von Schiller (1759-1805).

SPEECH OF THE MAID OF ORLEANS.

Archbishop.

Who art thou, wonderful and holy Maid ?
What favoured region bore thee ?   What blest pair,
Beloved of heaven, may claim thee as their child ?

Johanna.

Most Reverend Father.   I am named Johanna :
I am a shepherd's lowly daughter, born
In Dom Remi, a village of my king,
Included in the diocese of Toul,
And, from a child, I kept my father's sheep.
And much and frequently I heard them tell
Of the strange islanders, who o'er the sea
Had come to make us slaves, and on us force
A foreign lord, who loveth not the people ;
How the great city, Paris, they had seized,
And had usurped dominion o'er the realm.
Then, earnestly God's Mother I implored
To save us from the shame of foreign chains,
And to preserve to us our lawful king.
Not distant from my native village stands
An ancient Image of the Virgin Blest,
To which the pious pilgrims oft repaired ;
Hard by a holy oak, of blessed power,
Standeth, far famed through wonders manifold.
Beneath the oak's broad shade I loved to sit,
Tending my flock—my heart still drew me there,

And, if by chance among the desert hills
A lambkin strayed, 'twas shown me in a dream,
When in the shadow of this oak I slept.

And once, when through the night, beneath this
    tree,
In pious adoration I had sat,
Resisting sleep, the Holy One appeared,
Bearing a sword and banner, otherwise
Clad like a shepherdess ; and thus she spake :
' 'Tis I.   Arise, Johanna ; leave thy flock :
The Lord appoints thee to another task.
Receive this banner.   Gird thee with this sword :
Therewith exterminate my people's foes.
Conduct to Rheims thy royal master's son ;
And crown him with the kingly diadem.'
And I made answer : ' How may I presume
To undertake such deeds, a tender maid,
Unpractised in the dreadful art of war ? '
And she replied : ' A maiden pure and chaste
Achieves whate'er on earth is glorious,
If she to earthly love ne'er yields her heart.
Look upon me, a Virgin, like thyself :
I to the Christ, the Lord Divine, gave birth,
And am myself divine.'   Mine eyelids then
She touched ; and, when I upward turned my
    gaze,
Heaven's wide expanse was filled with angel-boys,
Who bore white lilies in their hands, while tones
Of sweetest music floated through the air.

And thus, on three successive nights appeared
The Holy One, and cried : ' Arise, Johanna ;
The Lord appoints thee to another task.'
And, when the third night she revealed herself,
Wrathful she seemed, and chiding spake these words:
' Obedience, woman's duty here on earth ;
Severe endurance is her heavy doom ;
She must be purified through discipline ;
Who serveth here is glorified above.'
While thus she spake, she let her shepherd garb
Fall from her, and as the Queen of Heaven stood
    forth,
Enshrined in radiant light, whilst golden clouds
Upbore her slowly to the realms of bliss.

Archbishop.

Before divine credentials such as these
Each doubt of earthly prudence must subside,
Her deeds attest the truth of what she speaks ;
For, God alone such wonders can achieve.

F. W. FABER (1814-1863).

THE AGED LANCELOT'S PRAYER-LIKE HYMN
AFTER HIS ABSOLUTION.

See, see, how evening's sloping shadows grow
    Upon the massy nave, and all the stone
    Is flecked with little clouds of colour, thrown
From the west window ; on the ground they go,
Silently creeping eastward, while the air
    Thickens within the choir, and so conceals

The altar, whose benignant Presence there
The slowly rocking lamp alone reveals.
Ah me, how still.   Our Lady's Vesper-song
Hath died away amid the choral throng ;
But, the pure-visaged moon, that climbs elate
The throne of day, now strikes with trembling
light
The painted lattice, where the live-long night
Saint Mary chaunts her lone ' Magnificat.'

Hail, Mary, hail : O Maiden-Mother, hail.
In thankfulness I lean upon the thought
Of thy mysterious chastities ; unsought
Comes the sweet faith thy prayers can never fail
In that high heaven where thou hast been assumed ;
And with this hope my spirit newly plumed
Strives upward, like a weary dove in sight
Of her lost refuge, steering by the light
Wherewith thy name hath silently illumined
The Church below, cheering the gradual night
The world hath forced upon the primal day
Of our sweet faith ; and I, on penance cast
Till patient yearning should retrieve the past,
May bless thee for the succour of thy ray.
The light is vocal, wavering on the glass :
The jewel midway in the braided hair,
The eyes, the lifted hand, are speaking there,
And o'er the lips the argent quiverings pass.
She sings ; she sings : but, thirsty silence drinks
The heavenly sound before its burden sinks
Into my listening ear.   Hail, Mary, hail :

Hail, thou that art the Haven of the heart
Accessible in all our moods ; a Veil
   Obscuring not, but gifted to impart
New aspects of the cross : though sin erase
   That Sign from heaven, before our downcast eyes,
   Which fall on thee, its sweet reflection lies
Like a soft shadow in a moon-lit place.
Hail, Mary, hail : O wondrous Mother, pray
To thy dear Son, who takes our sins away.

SIR WALTER SCOTT (1771-1832).

Ave Maria ; Maiden mild—
   Listen to a maiden's prayer ;
Thou canst hear though from the wild,
   Thou canst save amid despair.
Safe may we sleep beneath thy care,
   Though banished, outcast and reviled—
      Maiden, hear a maiden's prayer ;
      Mother, hear a suppliant child.
         Ave Maria.

Ave Maria ; Undefiled—
   The flinty couch we now must share
Shall seem with down of eider piled,
   If thy protection hover there.
The murky cavern's heavy air
   Shall breathe of balm, if thou hast smiled—
Then, Maiden, hear a maiden's prayer ;
   Mother, list a suppliant child.
         Ave Maria.

Ave Maria ; Stainless styled—
    Foul demons of the earth and air,
From this their wonted haunt exiled,
    Shall flee before thy presence fair.
We bow us to our lot of care,
    Beneath thy guidance reconciled—
Hear for a maid a maiden's prayer ;
    And for a father hear a child.
        Ave Maria.

DANTE GABRIEL ROSSETTI (1828-1882).

The lilies stand before her like a screen
    Through which, upon this warm and solemn day,
    God surely hears. For there she kneels to pray
Who wafts our prayers to God—Mary the Queen.
She was Faith's Present, parting what had been
    From what began with her, and is for aye.
    On either hand, God's twofold system lay :
With meek bowed face a Virgin prayed between.
So prays she, and the Dove flies in to her.
    And she has turned.   At the low porch is one
    Who looks as though deep awe made him to smile.
Heavy with heat the plants yield shadow there ;
    The loud flies cross each other in the sun ;
    And the aisled pillars meet the poplar-aisle.

FRANCIS THOMPSON (1860-1907).

Think, O sick toiler, when the night
Comes on thee, sad and infinite.

THE CORONATION OF THE VIRGIN

Fra Angelico

Think, sometimes, 'tis our own Lady
Spreads her own mantle over thee,

And folds the earth, a wearied thing,
Beneath its gentle shadowing ;

Then rest a little, and in deep
Forget to weep, forget to weep !

RUDYARD KIPLING (1865-).

Ah ! Mary, pierced with sorrow,
    Remember, reach and save
The soul that comes to-morrow
    Before the God that gave !
Since each was born of woman,
    For each at utter need,
True comrade and true foeman—
    Madonna, intercede !

LORD TENNYSON (1809-1892).

With one black shadow at its feet,
    The house thro' all the level shines,
Close-latticed to the brooding heat,
    And silent in its dusty vines :
A faint-blue ridge upon the right,
    An empty river-bed before,
    And shallows on a distant shore,
In glaring sand and inlets bright.

Y

But ' Ave Mary,' made she moan,
    And ' Ave Mary,' night and morn,
And ' Ah,' she sang, ' to be all alone,
    To live forgotten, and love forlorn.'

She, as her carol sadder grew,
    From brow and bosom slowly down
Through rosy taper fingers drew
    Her streaming curls of deepest brown
To left and right, and made appear
    Still-lighted in a secret shrine,
    Her melancholy eyes divine,
The home of woe without a tear.
        And ' Ave Mary,' was her moan,
        ' Madonna, sad is night and morn,'
    And, ' Ah,' she sang, ' to be all alone,
        To live forgotten, and love forlorn.'

Till all the crimson changed, and past
    Into deep orange o'er the sea,
Low on her knees herself she cast,
    Before Our Lady murmured she ;
Complaining, ' Mother, give me grace
    To help me of my weary load.'
    And on the liquid mirror glow'd
The clear perfection of her face.
        ' Is this the form,' she made her moan,
            ' That won his praises night and morn ? '
        And ' Ah,' she said, ' but I wake alone,
            I sleep forgotten, I wake forlorn.'

    .   .   .   .   .   .

Dreaming, she knew it was a dream :
   She felt he was and was not there.
She woke : the babble of the stream
   Fell, and, without, the steady glare
Shrank one sick willow sere and small.
    The river-bed was dusty-white ;
    And all the furnace of the light
Struck up against the blinding wall.
      She whisper'd, with a stifled moan,
        More inward than at night or morn,
     ' Sweet Mother, let me not here alone
       Live forgotten, and die forlorn.'

.   .   .   .   .

But sometimes in the falling day
   An image seem'd to pass the door,
To look into her eyes and say,
   ' But thou shalt be alone no more.'
And flaming downward over all
   From heat to heat the day decreased,
   And slowly rounded to the east
The one black shadow from the wall.
     ' The day to night,' she made her moan,
      ' The day to night, the night to morn,
    And day and night I am left alone
      To live forgotten, and love forlorn.'

At eve a dry cicala sung,
   There came a sound as of the sea ;
Backward the lattice-blind she flung,
   And lean'd upon the balcony.

There all in spaces rosy-bright
  Large Hesper glitter'd on her tears,
  And deepening thro' the silent spheres
Heaven over Heaven rose the night.
    And weeping then she made her moan,
      ' The night comes on that knows not
        morn,
      When I shall cease to be all alone,
        To live forgotten, and love forlorn.'

ARTHUR SHEARLY CRIPPS (1869-).

  Our earth grows virgin cool and calm,
  Humble and simple, kind and new,
  In bosomed hills the red sun falls—
  And all at once the low bell calls
  ' Now and in our last hour be true ! '

  Mother of earth, a child you stood
  (The March eve glimmers now and then),
  Shechinah of a Sunset fell
  Into your bosom there to dwell
  And rise to East for wandering men !

  O you that know our pit-falls dark,
  While high on heavenly hills you stand,
  Come, Day-Shine, at the end of day !
  As God stoop'd to you all the way,
  Stoop to us—husht and bright and bland !

Felicia D. Hemans (1793-1835).

ITALIAN GIRL'S HYMN TO THE VIRGIN.

In the deep hour of dreams,
Through the dark woods, and past the moaning sea,
And by the star-light gleams—
Mother of Sorrows, lo, I come to thee.

Unto thy shrine I bear
Night-blowing flowers, like my own heart, to lie
All, all unfolded there,
Beneath the meekness of thy pitying eye.

For thou, that once didst move,
In thy still beauty, through an early home,
Thou knowest the grief, the love,
The fear of woman's soul—to thee I come.

Many and sad and deep
Were the thoughts folded in thy silent breast ;
Thou, too, couldst watch and weep—
Hear, gentlest Mother, hear a heart opprest.

There is a wandering bark
Bearing one from me o'er the restless wave :
Oh, let thy soft eye mark
His course : be with him, Holiest, guide and save.

My soul is on that way ;
My thoughts are travellers, o'er the waters dim ;
Through the long weary day
I walk, o'ershadowed by vain dreams of him.

Aid him ; and me, too, aid ;
Oh, 'tis not well, this earthly love's excess :
On thy weak child is laid
The burden of too deep a tenderness.

Too much o'er him is poured
My being's hope—scarce leaving heaven a part ;
Too fearfully adored,
Oh, make not him the chastener of my heart.

I tremble with a sense
Of grief to be : I hear a warning low :
Sweet Mother, call me hence ;
This wild idolatry must end in woe.

The troubled joys of life,
Love's lightning happiness, my soul hath known ;
And, worn with feverish strife,
Would fold its wings : take back, take back thine own.

Hark, how the wind swept by :
The tempest's voice comes rolling o'er the wave :
Hope of the sailor's eye
And maiden's heart, blest Mother, guide and save.

NOVALIS (1772-1801).

In many a form I see thee oft,
    O Mary, beauteously portrayed ;
But never with such semblance soft
    As to my soul thou cam'st arrayed.

I only know, the world's annoy,
   Since then, like transient dream doth fade,
And an eternal heaven of joy
   My spirit hath its dwelling made.

GERALD GRIFFIN (1803-1840).

As the mute nightingale of closest groves
   Lies hid at noon, but, when day's piercing eye
   Is locked in night, with full heart beating high
Poureth her plain-song o'er the light she loves ;
So, Virgin Ever-pure and Ever-blest,
   Moon of religion, from whose radiant face
   Reflected streams the light of heavenly grace
On broken hearts, by contrite thoughts oppressed :
So, Mary, they who justly feel the weight
   Of Heaven's offended Majesty, implore
   Thy reconciling aid, with suppliant knee :
Of sinful man, O sinless Advocate,
   To thee they turn, nor him they less adore ;
   'Tis still his light they love, less dreadful seen
     in thee.

GIROLAMO SAVONAROLA (1452-1498).

   O Star of Galilee,
   Shining o'er this earth's dark sea,
   Shed thy glorious light on me.

   Queen of Clemency and Love
   Be my Advocate above,
   And, through Christ, all sin remove.

When the angel called thee blest,
And with transports filled thy breast,
'Twas thy Lord became thy guest.

Earth's purest Creature thou,
In the heavens exulting now,
With a halo round thy brow.

Beauty beams in every trace
Of the Virgin-Mother's face,
Full of glory and of grace—

A Beacon to the just,
To the sinner Hope and Trust,
Joy of the angel-host.

Ever-glorified, thy throne
Is where thy blessed Son
Doth reign : through him alone

All pestilence shall cease,
And sin and strife decrease,
And the kingdom come of peace.

GOETHE (from *Faust*) (1749-1832).

DOCTOR MARIANUS, *in the highest, purest cell.*

Here is the prospect free,
The soul uplifted.
Yonder float women by,
Heavenward drifted.

Glorious amidst them e'en,
Crownèd with the star-shine,
See I high Heaven's Queen
Radiant afar shine.

Thou that reignest as Thy due,
Lady, of Thy pleasure,
Let me Thine arcana view
In the vaulted azure !
Sanction what man's breast doth move,
Reverent and tender,
And with holy bliss of love
Nigher Thee doth render.

All invincible we grow
When august Thou willest,
Tempered straightway is the glow
If our hearts Thou stillest.
Virgin pure from stain of earth,
Mother honour-thronèd,
Chosen Queen, and peer by birth
With the Godhead ownèd !

Clouds wreathe the splendour
Frail as a feather.
Penitents tender
Are they, together
Drinking the ether,
Round her knees pleading,
Pardon sore-needing.

z

CHORUS OF PENITENT WOMEN.

To heights art soaring
Of Realms Eternal !
Hear us imploring
Peerless, Supernal,
Gracious, Maternal !

EDGAR ALLAN POE (1809-1849).

At morn, at noon, at twilight dim,
Maria, thou hast heard my hymn :
In joy and woe, in good and ill,
Mother of God, be with me still.
When the hours flew brightly by,
And not a cloud obscured the sky,
My soul, lest it should truant be,
Thy grace did guide to thine and thee.
Now, when storms of fate o'ercast
Darkly my present and my past,
Let my future radiant shine
With sweet hopes of thee and thine.

LORD BYRON (1788-1824).

Ave, Maria ; o'er the earth and sea,
That heavenliest hour of heaven is worthiest thee.
Ave, Maria ; blessed be the hour,
    The time, the clime, the spot, where I so oft
Have felt that moment in its fullest power
    Sink o'er the earth so beautiful and soft,

While swung the deep bell in the distant tower,
  Or the faint dying day-hymn stole aloft,
And not a breath crept through the rosy air,
And yet, the forest leaves seemed stirred with prayer.

Ave, Maria ; 'tis the hour of prayer ;
  Ave, Maria ; 'tis the hour of love ;
Ave, Maria ; may our spirits dare
  Look up to thine and to thy Son's above ;
Ave, Maria ; oh, that face so fair ;
  Thou downcast eyes beneath the Almighty Dove—
What though 'tis but a pictured image strike,
That painting is no idol—'tis too like.

THOMAS MOORE (1779-1852).

  When evening shades are falling
    O'er ocean's sunny sleep,
  To pilgrims' hearts recalling
    Their home beyond the deep ;
  When rest, o'er all descending,
    The shores with gladness smile,
  And lutes, their echoes blending,
    Are heard from isle to isle :
      Then, Mary, Star of the Sea,
      We pray, we pray, to thee.

  The noon-day tempest over,
    Now ocean toils no more,
  And wings of halcyons hover,
    Where all was strife before ;

Oh, thus may life, in closing
Its short tempestuous day,
Beneath heaven's smile reposing,
Shine all its storms away :
Thus, Mary, Star of the Sea,
We pray, we pray, to thee.

CARDINAL NEWMAN (1801-1890).

O my Lord and Saviour, support me in my last hour
by the strong arms of Thy Sacraments, and the fragrance of Thy consolations. Let Thy absolving word
be said over me, and the holy oil sign and seal me ; and
let Thine own Body be my food, and Thy Blood my
sprinkling ; and let Thy Mother, Mary, come to me,
and my angel whisper peace to me, and Thy glorious
saints and my own dear patrons smile on me, that in
and through them all I may die, as I desire to live, in
Thy Church, in Thy faith, and in Thy love. Amen.

XII

THE WITNESS OF THE AGES

Behold, from henceforth all generations shall call me blessed.—
St. Luke i. 48.

St. Cyril of Alexandria (315-386).

We salute thee, O treasure worthy of veneration,
that belongest to all mankind.

St. Ambrose (340-397).

Christ before the Virgin—Christ from the Virgin—
born indeed of the Father before all ages, but born
of the Virgin for the sake of the ages.

E. P. Ryder (1886).

Thine is the face that, while the centuries glide
  Into the silent chambers of the past,
Remains unchanged, unmoved by time, or tide.

Alice Meynell (1850-1922).

  We too (one cried), we too,
  We the unready, the perplexed, the cold,
  Must shape the Eternal in our thoughts anew,
    Cherish, possess, enfold.

Thou sweetly, we in strife,
It is our passion to conceive Him thus
In mind, in sense, within our house of life ;
    That seed is locked for us.

We must affirm our Son
From the ambiguous Nature's difficult speech,
Gather in darkness that resplendent One,
    Close as our grasp can reach.

Nor shall we ever rest
From this our task.   An hour sufficed for thee
Thou innocent !   He lingers in the breast
    Of our humanity.

ADELAIDE A. PROCTER (1825-1864).

It is one long chaplet of memories,
    Tender and true and sweet,
That gleam in the past and the distance
    Like lamps that burn at her feet ;
Like stars that will shine for ever,
    For time cannot touch, or stir
The graces that Mary has given,
    Or the trust that we give to her.
Past griefs are perished and over ;
    Past joys have vanished and died ;
Past loves are fled and forgotten ;
    Past hopes have been laid aside ;
Past fears have faded in daylight ;
    Past sins have melted in tears—
One love and remembrance only
    Seems alive in those dead old years.

So, wherever I look in the distance,
    And whenever I turn to the past,
There is always a Shrine of Mary
    Each brighter still than the last.

CARDINAL NEWMAN (1801-1890).

'Our God was carried in the womb of Mary,' said Ignatius, who was martyred A.D. 106. 'The Word of God,' says Hippolytus, 'was carried in that Virgin frame.' 'The Maker of all,' says Amphilochius, 'is born of a Virgin.' 'She did compass without circumscribing the Sun of justice—the Everlasting is born,' says Chrysostom. 'God dwelt in the womb,' says Proclus. 'When thou hearest that God speaks from the bush,' asks Theodotus, 'in the bush seest thou not the Virgin?' Cassian says, 'Mary bore her Author.' 'The One God only-begotten,' says Hilary, 'is introduced into the womb of a Virgin.' 'The Everlasting,' says Ambrose, 'came into the Virgin.' 'The closed gate,' says Jerome, 'by which alone the Lord God of Israel enters, is the Virgin Mary.' 'That man from heaven,' says Capriolus, 'is God conceived in the womb.' 'He is made in thee,' says St. Augustine, 'who made thee.'

The current of thought in those early ages did uniformly tend to make much of the Blessed Virgin and to increase her honours, not to circumscribe them. Little jealousy was shown of her in those times; but, when any such niggardliness of affection occurred, then one Father or other fell upon the offender, with zeal, not to say with fierceness. Thus St. Jerome inveighs against Helvidius ; thus St. Epiphanius denounces Apollinaris, St. Cyril Nestorius and St. Ambrose, Bonosus ; on the other hand, each successive insult offered to her by individual adversaries did but bring out more fully the intimate sacred affection with which Christendom regarded her. 'She was alone, and wrought the world's salvation and conceived the redemption of all,' says Ambrose ; 'she had so great grace, as not only to preserve virginity herself, but to confer it on those whom she visited.' 'She is the rod out of the stem of Jesse,' says St. Jerome, 'and the Eastern gate through which the High Priest alone goes in and out, which still is ever shut.' 'She is the wise woman,' says Nilus, 'who hath clad believers from the fleece of the Lamb born of her, with the clothing of incorruption, and delivered them from their spiritual nakedness.' 'She is the mother of life, of beauty, of majesty, the morning star,' according to Antiochus. 'The mystical new heavens,' 'the heavens carrying the Divinity,' 'the fruitful vine,' 'by whom we are translated from death unto life,' according to St. Ephrem. 'The manna, which is delicate, bright, sweet, and virgin, which, as though coming from heaven, has poured down on all the people of the Churches a food pleasanter than honey,' according to St. Maximus.

Basil of Seleucia says, that 'she shines out above all the martyrs as the sun above the stars, and that she mediates between God and men.' 'Run through all creation in your thought,' says Proclus, 'and see if there be one equal or superior to the Holy Virgin, Mother of God.' 'Hail, Mother, clad in light, of the

THE CORONATION OF THE VIRGIN
Velazquez

light which sets not,' says Theodotus, or some one else at Ephesus ; ' hail, all undefiled mother of holiness ; hail, most pellucid fountain of the life-giving stream.' And St. Cyril too at Ephesus, ' Hail, Mary, Mother of God, majestic common-treasure of the whole world, the lamp unquenchable, the crown of virginity, the sceptre of orthodoxy, the indissoluble temple, the dwelling of the Illimitable, Mother and Virgin, through whom He in the holy gospels is called blessed who cometh in the name of the Lord.'

THE VENERABLE BEDE (673-735).

By the grace of God, if we always keep in mind the acts and words of the Blessed Mary, we shall always persevere in the observance of the works of a pure and virtuous life. It is a most excellent and useful custom that has grown up in the Holy Church, that Mary's hymn is sung by all daily at Vespers—*cum psalmodia Vespertinae laudis.* Thus the minds of the faithful are stirred, by a more frequent memory of our Lord's Incarnation, to a greater devotion, and confirmed in solid virtue by the frequent thought of the example of His Mother.

ROBERT BRIDGES, POET LAUREATE (1844-).

NOEL: CHRISTMAS EVE, 1913.
Pax hominibus bonæ voluntatis.

A frosty Christmas Eve
   when the stars were shining
Fared I forth alone
   where westward falls the hill,

2 A

And from many a village
   in the water'd valley
Distant music reach'd me
   peals of bells aringing :
The constellated sounds
   ran sprinkling on earth's floor
As the dark vault above
   with stars was spangled o'er.

Then sped my thought to keep
   that first Christmas of all
When the shepherds watching
   by their folds ere the dawn
Heard music in the fields
   and marveling could not tell
Whether it were angels
   or the bright stars singing.

Now blessed be the tow'rs
   that crown England so fair
That stand up strong in prayer
   unto God for our souls :
Blessed be their founders
   (said I) an' our country folk
Who are ringing for Christ
   in the belfries to-night
With arms lifted to clutch
   the rattling ropes that race
Into the dark above
   and the mad romping din.

But to me heard afar
  it was starry music
Angels' song, comforting
  as the comfort of Christ
When he spake tenderly
  to his sorrowful flock :
The old words came to me
  by the riches of time
Mellow'd and transfigured
  as I stood on the hill
Heark'ning in the aspect
  of th' eternal silence.

AMY K. CLARKE.

Through the Uncreated,
  Uncleft, Untrod,
Breathed for a moment
  Sorrow of God.

And lo ! it fell starlike,—
  Trembling to cease
In His Infinite gladness
  Infinite peace.

Out of that tremor
  Time was made,
Worlds crept into being
  Young and afraid.

Slowly, by beauty
  His creatures grew wise,
Slow dawned its wonder
  On opening eyes.

Men watched adoring
  His waters roll,
Deep flowed His colours
  Through sense and soul.

Moan of creation,
  Rapture that stirs—
Blindly they learned it,
  Years upon years :

Till clearly one spirit
  Cried on His Name
From all her lovely
  And earthly frame.

Light could not veil it,
  Nor darkness dim,
Flesh but receive it—
  Vision of Him.

Deep sunk His answer,
  His Word that sufficed—
Out of her Body
  Cometh His Christ.

MONSIGNOR BARRY (1849-).

MARY'S TRIUMPH.

That picture was a new creation. The splendour of
the vision came back, the heavenly dyes of angelic
raiment, the brightness of the martyrs' crimson, the
golden emerald of the far-off gleaming gates. Most
wonderful of all, the countenance that had been lost
was visible once more, drawing all eyes to it, in calm
unconscious beauty, already enlightened, as it should
seem, with the glory that falls from the Great White
Throne. It was not the likeness of any human face ;
in it there was unspeakable innocence, humility, gladness, a pure light on the brow, a tenderness in the
gentle eyes, a majesty blent with meekness in the
pose of the head, which bore its diadem of glittering
stones as if they had been flowers. The sense of
eternal triumph might be discerned in the movement
of that glorious procession, as it swept through the
air and mounted towards the stars of God. Quitting
the world of clouds it had attained the region of trans-
parent light ; nor was there a reminiscence of pain
or grief on any countenance. The martyrs seemed
springing to a new and divine life out of the wine-
dark tide in which they had been plunged. The
Cherubim, with the rose of everlasting youth upon
their wings, soared upward like lambent fire.

JOHN RUSKIN (1819-1900).

After the most careful examination, neither as adversary nor friend, of the influence of Catholicity for good and evil, I am persuaded that the worship of the Madonna has been one of the noblest and most vital graces, and has never been otherwise than productive of true holiness of life and purity of character. There has probably not been an innocent cottage home throughout the length and breadth of Europe during the whole period of vital Christianity, in which the imagined presence of the Madonna has not given sanctity to the humblest duties, and comfort to the sorest trials of the lives of women ; and every brightest and loftiest achievement of the arts and strength of manhood has been the fulfilment of the prophecy of the Israelite maiden, ' He that is mighty hath magnified me and holy is His Name.'

W. E. H. LECKY (1838-1903).

The world is governed by its ideals, and seldom or never has there been one which has exercised a more profound or, upon the whole, a more salutary influence than the medieval conception of the Virgin. For the first time woman was elevated to her rightful position, and the sanctity of weakness was recognised as well as the sanctity of sorrow. No longer the slave or the toy of man, no longer associated only with ideas of degradation and of sensuality, woman rose, in the person of the Virgin Mother, into a new sphere and became the object of a reverential homage of which antiquity had no conception. Love was idealised. The moral charm and beauty of female excellence were fully felt. A new type of character was called into being, a new kind of admiration was fostered. Into a harsh and ignorant and benighted age this ideal type infused a conception of gentleness and of purity unknown to the proudest civilisation of the past. In the pages of living tenderness which many a monkish writer has left in honour of his celestial patron, in the millions who in many lands and in many ages have sought with no barren desire to mould their characters into her image, in those holy maidens who, for love of Mary, have separated themselves from all the glories and pleasures of the world to seek in fastings and vigils and humble charity to render themselves worthy of her benediction, in the new sense of honour, in the chivalrous respect, in the softening of manners, in the refinement of tastes displayed in all the walks of society : in these, and in many other ways, we detect its influence. All that was best in Europe clustered around it, and it is the origin of the purest elements of our civilisation.

Bishop Ullathorne (1806-1889).

The words of the Almighty resound across the ages from the book of Genesis. Amidst the cries of woe and distress from our apostate progenitors, amidst God's terrible denunciations of their crime, amidst the tempest of maledictions which come pouring on the

world, amidst the awful curses with which the wrath
of the Eternal overwhelms the infernal author of our
ruin, there breathe tender notes of His love for man,
which prelude the solution of the world's catastrophe.
They announce the coming of a new Mother, a Mother
of life, a Mother who, as well as her offspring, shall be
victorious over the devil, and shall pass untouched by
his evil powers to the fulfilment of her great office.
And the first intimation of the Gospel of peace is the
proclamation of that Immaculate Mother : ' I will
put enmities between thee and the woman, and thy
seed and her seed.'

And as the Old Testament begins by proclaiming
her, so the New Testament begins with words ad-
dressed to her from heaven : ' Hail, full of grace.
The Lord is with thee ' ; that is, as an ancient Father
writes, ' Hail, formed in grace.' Hail, in whom God
always dwells. Hail, whose grace is co-extensive with
thy nature. And thus from the beginning the truth
was sown both in the minds of the Fathers and in the
hearts of the faithful.

ROBERT STEPHEN HAWKER (1803-1875).

It flowed, like light, from the voice of God
    Silent and calm and fair ;
It shows where the child and the parent trod,
    In the soft and evening air.
' Look at that spring, my father dear,
    Where the white blossoms fell :
Why is it always bright and clear ?
And why, the Lady's Well ? '

'Once on a time, my own sweet child,
    There dwelt across the sea
A lovely Mother, meek and mild,
    From blame and blemish free.
And Mary was her blessèd name,
    In every land adored :
Its very sound deep love should claim
    From all who love their Lord.
A child was hers—a heavenly birth,
    As pure as pure could be :
He had no father of the earth,
    The Son of God was he.
He came down to her from above,
    He died upon the cross :
We ne'er can do for him, my love,
    What he hath done for us.
And so, to make his praise endure,
    Because of Jesus' fame,
Our fathers called things bright and pure
    By his fair Mother's name.
She is the Lady of the Well—
    Her memory was meant
With lily and with rose to dwell
    By waters innocent.'

LEWIS MORRIS (1833-1907).

Fair Motherhood, by every childish tongue
Thy eulogy is sung.
In every passing age
The theme of seer and sage :

2 B

The painters saw thee in a life-long dream ;
The painters, who have left a world more fair
Than ever days of nymph and goddess were—
Blest company, who, now for centuries,
Have fixed the Virgin-Mother for our eyes—
The painters saw thee sitting, brown or fair,
Under the Tuscan vines, or colder northern air ;
They saw pure love transform thy peasant gaze ;
They saw thy reverent eyes, thy young amaze,
And left thee Queen of Heaven, wearing a crown
Of glory ; and abased at thy sweet breast,
Spurning his robes of kingship down,
The Child-God laid at rest.

They found thee, and they fixed thee for our eyes ;
But, every day that goes
Before the gazer, new Madonnas rise.
What matter, if the cheek show not the rose,
Nor look divine is there, nor queenly grace ?
The mother's glory lights the homely face.
In every land beneath the circling sun
Thy praise is never done.
Whatever men may doubt, they put their trust in
    thee ;
Rude souls and coarse, to whom virginity
Seems a dead thing and cold.
So always was it, from the days of old ;
So shall it be, while yet our race doth last ;
Though truth be sought no more and faith be past,
Still, till all hope of heaven be dead,
Thy praises shall be said.

W. CHATTERTON DIX (1837-1898).

Forgive, great Mother, all the years
    Wherein I passed thee by unknown :
Forgive the weak, unworthy fears
    Of faithlessness to Jesùs' throne.

I know Him better now and thee,
    I know Him and I love thee more
Than in those days, not shadow-free,
    When still I stood outside the door :

Outside the door of full content,
    When only through the opened gate
I fancied what that fulness meant
    Which in God's time should satiate.

But now I know thee ; yet, how faint
    My love and my devotion seem :
As if soft living framed the saint,
    And feeble love won Christ's esteem.

Men say that loving thee, I dim
    The glory of thy Son Divine,
But otherwise I learn of Him,
    And call thee His, and find thee mine.

His—for what mother who could own
    As thou, a Son and Saviour dear ?
Mine—for in Him still fairer grown,
    I find thee, ever, ever near.

H. W. Longfellow (1807-1882).

This is indeed the Blessèd Mary's land,
Virgin and Mother of our dear Redeemer.
All hearts are touched and softened at her name ;
Alike the bandit, with the bloody hand,
The priest, the prince, the scholar, and the peasant,
The man of deeds, the visionary dreamer,
Pay homage to her as one ever present.
And even as children, who have much offended
A too indulgent father, in great shame,
Penitent, and yet, not daring unattended
To go into his presence, at the gate
Speak with their sister, and confiding wait
Till she goes in before and intercedes ;
So, men, repenting of their evil deeds,
And yet, not venturing rashly to draw near
With their requests an angry father's ear,
Offer to her their prayers and their confession,
And she for them in heaven makes intercession.
And, if our faith had given us nothing more
Than this Example of all Womanhood,
So mild, so merciful, so strong, so good,
So patient, peaceful, loyal, loving, pure—
This were enough to prove it higher and truer
Than all the creeds the world had known before.

Virgin, who lovest the poor and lonely,
If the loud cry of a mother's heart

Can ever ascend to where thou art,
Into thy blessed hands and holy
Receive my prayer of praise and thanksgiving.
Let the hands that bore our Saviour bear it
Into the awful presence of God ;
For thy feet with holiness are shod,
And, if thou bearest it, he will hear it.

AUBREY THOMAS DE VERE (1814-1902).

As children when, with heavy tread,
   Men sad of face, unseen before,
Have borne away their mother dead—
   So stand the nations thine no more.

From room to room those children roam,
   Heart-stricken by the unwonted black :
Their house no longer seems their home :
   They search ; yet know not what they lack.

Years pass : self-will and passion strike
   Their roots more deeply day by day ;
Old kinsmen sigh ; and ' how unlike,'
   Is all the tender neighbours say.

And yet, at moments, like a dream,
   A mother's image o'er them flits :
Like hers, their eyes a moment beam ;
   The voice grows soft, the brow unknits.

Such, Mary, are the realms once thine
    That know no more thy golden reign :
Hold forth from heaven thy Babe Divine ;
    Oh, make thine orphans thine again.

CHRISTINA ROSSETTI (1830-1894).

They have brought gold and spices to my King,
    Incense and precious stuffs and ivory :
O holy Mother mine, what can I bring
    That so my Lord may deign to look on me ?
They sing a sweeter song than I can sing,
    All crowned and glorified exceedingly :
I, bound on earth, weep for my trespassing,—
    They sing the song of love in heaven, set free.
Then answered me my Mother, and her voice
    Spake to my heart, yea answered in my heart :
' Sing, saith He to the heavens, to earth, Rejoice :
Thou also lift thy heart to Him above :
    He seeks not thine, but thee such as thou art,
For lo His banner over thee is Love.'

DIGBY MACKWORTH DOLBEN (1848-1867).

Tell us, tell us, holy shepherds,
    What at Bethlehem you saw.—

' Very God of Very God
   Asleep amid the straw.'

Tell us, tell us, all ye faithful,
   What this morning came to pass
At the awful elevation
   In the Canon of the Mass.—
' Very God of Very God,
   By whom the worlds were made,
In silence and in helplessness
   Upon the altar laid.'

Tell us, tell us, wondrous Jesu,
   What has drawn Thee from above
To the manger and the altar.—
   All the silence answers—Love.
Through the roaring streets of London
   Thou art passing, hidden Lord,
Uncreated, Consubstantial,
   In the seventh heaven adored.

As of old the ever-Virgin
   Through unconscious Bethlehem
Bore Thee, not in glad procession,
   Jewelled robe and diadem ;
Not in pomp and not in power,
   Onward to Nativity,
Shrined but in the tabernacle
   Of her sweet Virginity.

Still Thou goest by in silence,
　　Still the world cannot receive,
　Still the poor and weak and weary
　　Only, worship and believe.

F. W. Faber (1814-1863).

O purest of creatures ! sweet Mother ! sweet Maid !
The one spotless womb wherein Jesus was laid !
Dark night hath come down on us, Mother ! and we
Look out for thy shining, sweet Star of the Sea !

Deep night hath come down on this rough-spoken
　　world,
And the banners of darkness are boldly unfurled :
And the tempest-tost Church—all her eyes are on
　　thee,
They look to thy shining, sweet Star of the Sea !

He gazed on thy soul ; it was spotless and fair ;
For the empire of sin—it had never been there ;
None had e'er owned thee, dear Mother, but He,
And He blessed thy clear shining, sweet Star of the
　　Sea !

Earth gave Him one lodging ; 'twas deep in thy
　　breast,
And God found a home where the sinner finds rest ;
His home and His hiding-place, both were in thee ;
He was won by thy shining, sweet Star of the Sea !

Oh, blissful and calm was the wonderful rest
That thou gavest thy God in thy virginal breast ;
For the heaven He left He found heaven in thee,
And He shone in thy shining, sweet Star of the Sea !

COVENTRY PATMORE (1823-1896).

Gaze without blame
Ye in whom living love yet blushes for dead shame.
There of pure Virgins none
Is fairer seen,
Save One,
Than Mary.
Gaze without doubt or fear
Ye to whom generous Love, by any name, is dear.
Love makes the life to be
A fount perpetual of virginity ;
For, lo, the Elect,
Of generous love, how named soe'er, affect
Nothing but God,
Or meditate or direct
Nothing but God,
The Husband of the Heavens :
And who Him Love, in potence great or small,
Are, one and all,
Heirs of the Palace glad,
And inly clad
With the bridal robes of ardour virginal.

2 C

Mother, who lead'st me still by unknown ways,
Giving the gifts I know not how to ask,
Bless thou this work
Which, done, redeems my many wasted days,
Makes white the murk,
And crowns the few which thou wilt not dispraise.
Ora pro me !

Ave, Maria, gratia plena ; Dominus tecum : benedicta tu in mulieribus, et benedictus fructus ventris tui Jesus. Sancta Maria, Mater Dei, ora pro nobis peccatoribus, nunc et in hora mortis nostræ.   Amen.

ACKNOWLEDGMENTS

THE Editor desires to express his cordial thanks to the following Authors and Publishers for permission to include poems, translations, and prose extracts in this Anthology :—Dr. Robert Bridges and his Publisher, Sir John Murray ; Mr. Wilfrid Meynell for Alice Meynell and Francis Thompson ; Rev. John Fitzpatrick, O.M.I., for translations of 'Adeste, Fideles,' 'Stabat Mater Speciosa,' 'Stabat Mater Dolorosa,' 'Sacra Jam Splendent Decorata Lychnis' (Pope Leo XIII.), 'Te, Joseph, Celebrent,' and 'Iste, Quem Laeti,' and for 'My Lady is a fragrant Rose'; Messrs. Burns and Oates for the late Father Livius, C.SS.R., and Father T. E. Bridgett, for translations from the Early Fathers ; the late Father Hugh Benson, Father Tabb, Father Kent, O.S.C., H. N. Oxenham, Henry A. Rawes, John Tauler, and the late Wm. Chatterton Dix ; Sir Henry Newbolt for Mary Elizabeth Coleridge ; Mr. Selwyn Image ; Mr. G. K. Chesterton and his Publisher, Mr. Cecil Palmer ; Mr. Basil Blackwell for Rev. Arthur Cripps and Amy K. Clarke ; Mr. Stephen de Vere for the late Aubrey de Vere ; Laurence Housman ; Messrs. Macmillan and Co. Ltd. for Christina and Gabriel

Rossetti ; Messrs. Longmans, Green and Co. Ltd. for F. W. H. Myers, C. B. Cayley's translation of Petrarch's Ode, and the late Cardinal Newman ; Dom A. B. Kuypers for Prayer of Aedelwald, Book of Cerne ; Lord Tennyson ; Mr. Rudyard Kipling for 'Ah ! Mary, pierced with sorrow' from 'Hymn before Action,' 1896 ; 'Carmina Mariana,' privately printed by the late Mr. Orby Shipley, M.A., and now out of print, has been of much service ; Mrs. Katherine Tynan Hinkson ; Mr. T. T. Tucker for the late Edith Nesbit ; the family of the late Father Gerard Hopkins ; Sir E. A. Wallis Budge and the Medici Society for translation of Ethiopic Weddāsê Māryām ; Messrs. G. Bell and Sons for Coventry Patmore ; Evelyn Underhill for translation of 'O Queen of all Courtesy' by Jacoponi da Todi ; and to Mr. Alfred Noyes, C.B.E., for 'Slumber-Songs of the Madonna.'

If after much care to discover owners of copyrights he has unwittingly missed any one or failed to acknowledge non-copyright material, he offers sincere apologies to all concerned.

ALPHABETICAL LIST OF AUTHORS
AND NOTES OF REFERENCE

Printed in Great Britain by T. and A. Constable Ltd.
at the University Press, Edinburgh

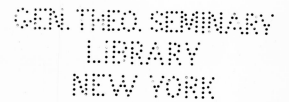